zuch frice casserole

zuchinni -

chicken delight

casserole topping

D0399379

green

p 47

p 49

p 49

Contents

INTRODUCTION

I grew up on a farm in Illinois with my Parents and Two Sisters. We walked to the Old Country School everyday, along with a few other children. The School had one classroom for all eight classes and one teacher who taught all classes. Since we didn't live far from School, we walked home for lunch at noon. How we envied the other kids who walked a long way to School, because they got to bring their lunch. Since we felt so deprived, Mother would ease our pain once in a while and let us take our lunch and oh what fun, getting to eat with the other kids. The memory is still vivid in my mind of coming home from School to the aroma of freshly Home Made doughnuts Mother had made, a special treat to three hungry School girls. Well, graduation day came and I graduated with an honor. Yes, there were two of us and it was an honor to have a classmate who graduated with me!!!!

I have many Childhood memories. One of them was watching Mother, as she put the broom handle over the back of the chickens neck, getting ready for the big kill. What a scene for a youngster! After the chickens quit flopping, they were dipped into scalding water, so the feathers could be picked easily. Then the chickens were transferred to a sink of cold water. I remember standing by the sink watching the chickens being cut in preparation for the frying pan.

We had several cherry trees in our large yard. We girls helped pick cherries that were to be made into jelly and pies, some to be put in the Locker.

I found it quite interesting how Grandma and Mother would put an old quilt under the Mulberry tree and then shake the tree to get the Mulberries from the trees.

Dad was a grain farmer, although we had cows in the pasture. Mother liked to have a milk cow, as she enjoyed using the fresh cream and milk. What a treat for me, to enjoy a glass of warm milk straight from the cow. I'll have to admit, it sounded better then than now!!

My farm background and down to earth country living have contributed much to the desire and pleasure I have received from a Life of Cooking and Baking, collecting good recipes, a satisfaction I have found in pleasing family and friends.

In the writing of my Cookbook, I have written it with "Today's pace of Living" in mind, with practical, clearly stated recipes for foods you will enjoy preparing for family and friends, hoping it will become your trusted Kitchen Companion, the Cookbook you will turn to often for quick and easy cooking, just the "Lifesaver" you've been wanting.

Today's busy wife, Mother and Career Woman needs all the help in the kitchen she can get. It is my sincere desire that within these pages you will find recipes so appetizing that when you serve your friends, you are certain to hear, "what a delicious dish, may I have your recipe?"

Beverages

MICROWAVE HINTS

1. Place an open box of hardened brown sugar in the microwave oven with 1 cup hot water. Microwave at high for 1½ to 2 minutes for ½ pound or 2 to 3 minutes for 1 pound.
2. Soften hard ice cream by microwaving at 30% power. One pint will take 15 to 30 seconds; one quart, 30 to 45 seconds; and one-half gallon 45 seconds to one minute.
3. One stick of butter or margarine will soften in 1 minute when microwaved at 20% power.
4. Soften one 8-ounce package of cream cheese by microwaving at 30% power for 2 to 2½ minutes. One 3-ounce package of cream cheese will soften in 1½ to 2 minutes.
5. Thaw frozen orange juice right in the container. Remove the top metal lid. Place the opened container in the microwave and heat on high power 30 seconds for 6 ounces and 45 seconds for 12 ounces.
6. Thaw whipped topping...a 4½ ounce carton will thaw in 1 minute on the defrost setting. Whipped topping should be slightly firm in the center but it will blend well when stirred. Do not overthaw!
7. Soften jello that has set up too hard—perhaps you were to chill it until slightly thickened and forgot it. Heat on a low power setting for a very short time.
8. Dissolve gelatin in the microwave. Measure liquid in a measuring cup, add jello and heat. There will be less stirring to dissolve the gelatin.
9. Heat hot packs in a microwave oven. A wet finger tip towel will take about 25 seconds. It depends on the temperature of the water used to wet the towel.
10. To scald milk, cook 1 cup milk for 2-2½ minutes, stirring once each minute.
11. To make dry bread crumbs, cut 6 slices bread into ½-inch cubes. Microwave in 3-quart casserole 6-7 minutes, or until dry, stirring after 3 minutes. Crush in blender.
12. Refresh stale potato chips, crackers or other snacks of such type by putting a plateful in the microwave oven for about 30-45 seconds. Let stand for 1 minute to crisp. Cereals can also be crisped.
13. Melt almond bark for candy or dipping pretzels. One pound will take about 2 minutes, stirring twice. If it hardens while dipping candy, microwave for a few seconds longer.
14. Nuts will be easier to shell if you place 2 cups of nuts in a 1-quart casserole with 1 cup of water. Cook for 4 to 5 minutes and the nut meats will slip out whole after cracking the shell.
15. When thawing hamburger meat, the outside will many times begin cooking before the meat is completely thawed. Defrost for 3 minutes, then remove the outside portions that have defrosted. Continue defrosting the hamburger, taking off the defrosted outside portions at short intervals.
16. To drain the fat from hamburger while it is cooking in the microwave oven (one pound cooks in 5 minutes on high), cook it in a plastic colander placed inside a casserole dish.
17. Cubed meat and chopped vegetables will cook more evenly if cut uniformly.
18. When baking large cakes, brownies, or moist bars, place a juice glass in the center of the baking dish to prevent a soggy middle and ensure uniform baking throughout.
19. Since cakes and quick breads rise higher in a microwave oven, fill pans just half full of batter.
20. For stamp collectors: place a few drops of water on stamp to be removed from envelope. Heat in the microwave for 20 seconds and the stamp will come right off.
21. Using a round dish instead of a square one eliminates overcooked corners in baking cakes.
22. When preparing chicken in a dish, place meaty pieces around the edges and the bony pieces in the center of the dish.
23. Shaping meatloaf into a ring eliminates undercooked center. A glass set in the center of a dish can serve as the mold.
24. Treat fresh meat cuts for 15 to 20 seconds on high in the microwave oven. This cuts down on meat-spoiling types of bacteria.
25. A crusty coating of chopped walnuts surrounding many microwave-cooked cakes and quick breads enhances the looks and eating quality. Sprinkle a layer of medium finely chopped walnuts evenly onto the bottom and sides of a ring pan or Bundt cake pan. Pour in batter and microwave as recipe directs.
26. Do not salt foods on the surface as it causes dehydration (meats and vegetables) and toughens the food. Salt the meat after you remove it from the oven unless the recipe calls for using salt in the mixture.
27. Heat left-over custard and use it as frosting for a cake.
28. Melt marshmallow creme in the microwave oven. Half of a 7-ounce jar will melt in 35-40 seconds on high. Stir to blend.
29. Toast coconut in the microwave. Watch closely as it browns quickly once it begins to brown. Spread ½ cup coconut in a pie plate and cook for 3-4 minutes, stirring every 30 seconds after 2 minutes.
30. Place a cake dish up on another dish or on a roasting rack if you have difficulty getting the bottom of the cake done. This also works for potatoes and other foods that don't quite get done on the bottom.

BEVERAGES

"This is the day which the Lord hath made; we will rejoice and be glad in it."
Psalms 188:24

RED PUNCH

A lovely drink for all occasions.

6 bottles strawberry pop
1 large can pineapple juice

3 c. ginger ale

Mix pop and pineapple juice and chill in refrigerator. Add ginger ale before serving.

PARTY OR SHOWER PUNCH

"This punch can be made any color - even blue. The secret is to add your coloring to the liquid before adding the ice cream."

3 bottles lemon lime drink (such as
Bubble-Up)
1½ c. pineapple juice (or to your
taste)

Vanilla ice cream

Combine all ingredients.

Whenever you entertain the Bunch,
Always plan to have a punch

Mmmmm PUNCH

"Makes delicate white punch. May substitute other sherbet and ice cream flavors to vary color and taste, receives compliments."

1 qt. pineapple sherbet
1 qt. vanilla ice cream

24 oz. pineapple juice
3 (12 oz.) cans ginger ale

Soften sherbet and ice cream slightly. Mix in pineapple juice. Pour into punch bowl. Add ginger ale. Makes 1 medium bowl. Serves 25 to 30 punch cups.

TROPICAL FRUIT PUNCH

1 14 oz. can Hawaiian fruit drink
1 - 16 oz. can frozen lemon ade
1 - 16 oz. can frozen orange juice

1 - 16 oz. can frozen grape juice
1 qt. ginger ale
6 cups cold water

Combine juices with water. Pour in gingerale. An extra touch may be added, using orange slices and mint leaves.

SLUSH

Summed up in one word, "Luscious."

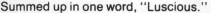

6 tart lemons
6 oranges or 1 small can frozen
   juice
6 large ripe bananas, mashed or
   crushed in blender

1 large can pineapple juice
6 c. water
5 c. sugar
2 large bottles 7-Up

Mix first four ingredients together. Heat water and sugar together until sugar dissolves, then cool. Mix with juices and pour into shallow containers and freeze. Remove from freezer about 30 minutes before serving and after thawing a bit, crush in blender and mix with the 7-Up.

HOMEMADE LEMONADE

¾ c. lemon juice (4 lemons)
¾ c. sugar

1 c. water
4 c. water

Squeeze lemons and reserve skins. In a saucepan, combine sugar, water and skins. Cover and simmer six minutes. Cool and discard skins. To this, add lemon juice, 4 cups water and more sugar as needed. Makes 4 to 5 servings.

SPICED TEA

2 c. Tang
1 c. instant tea
½ tsp. cloves

1 tsp. cinnamon
1 pkg. instant lemonade
½ c. sugar

Mix well, store in airtight jar. (Use 2 to 3 teaspoons per cup; add hot water.)

HOT CRANBERRY DRINK

For 22 cup percolator. Ideal for the holidays.

1½ qt. cranberry juice

2 qt. apple juice

In basket of percolator:

½ c. brown sugar
½ c. white sugar
½ tsp. salt

1½ tsp. whole cloves (optional)
4 to 5 sticks cinnamon, broken in
   pieces

Perk and serve.

APPLE CIDER PUNCH

6 cups apple cider
1 cinnamon stick
¼ t. nutmeg

¼ C. honey
3 T lemon juice
18 oz. can pineapple juice

Bring the cider and cinnamon stick to boil. Add the rest of ingredients.
Keep hot in crock pot.

HOT COCOA MIX

8 qt. box powdered milk
1 lb. Nestle's Quik

1 pound powdered sugar
6 oz. coffee creamer

Mix and store in dry place. To make, use ¼ cup of mix to 1 cup water.

HOLIDAY EGGNOG
(Creamy, rich and tasty)

1¾ oz. pkg. vanilla instant pudding
   mix
5½ c. cold milk
4 egg yolks, slightly beaten
1 tsp. vanilla

4 egg whites
4 Tbsp. sugar
1 env. topping mix, whipped
Sprinkle of nutmeg

Combine pudding mix with ¼ cup milk; blend in egg yolks. Stir in vanilla and remaining milk; beat with rotary beater for about 2 minutes. Beat egg whites until foamy. Add sugar, 2 tablespoons at a time, beating thoroughly after each addition. Beat until mixture forms stiff shiny peaks. Fold into pudding mixture; chill for several hours. Blend topping mix into eggnog just before serving. Sprinkle with nutmeg. Yields 8 cups or 16 servings.

GOLDEN GLOW PUNCH

3 oz. pkg. orange gelatin
1 c. boiling water
6 oz. can frozen pineapple juice
4 c. apple juice

3 c. cold water
3½ c. ginger ale, chilled
1 qt. sherbet (orange)

Dissolve gelatin in boiling water; stir in pineapple juice concentrate. Add apple juice and cold water. Add ginger ale and softened sherbet before serving. Makes 25 servings.

LIME PUNCH
(A very good refreshing punch!)

2 pkg. lime Kool-Aid (sweetened)
1 (46 oz.) can pineapple juice

1 qt. ginger ale
1 qt. lime sherbet

Mix together; chill. Add sherbet in chunks before serving. Serves 30.

HOT CIDER PUNCH

3 c. sweet cider
½ c. brown sugar

¼ c. butter
Cinnamon sticks (1 or 2)

In a saucepan, combine cider, brown sugar and butter; heat until melted. Add the cinnamon sticks; simmer 20 minutes.

Character is what are when we think that no one is watching us.

ORANGE FROST

The perfect brunch eye opener! Kids love it frozen as popsicles.

1 (6 oz.) can frozen orange juice
    concentrate
1 c. milk
1 c. water

½ c. sugar
1¼ tsp. vanilla
12 ice cubes

1. Mix all ingredients except ice, together in blender.
2. Add a few ice cubes at a time, beating at high speed until all ice cubes have been crushed.
Serve immediately.

Note: Garnish with a sprig of mint (optional).

TOMATO JUICE COCKTAIL

1 peck ripe tomatoes (about 12½
    lb.)
8 small onions
4 sweet peppers

Sprig of parsley or 1 tsp.
2 cloves garlic
2 hot peppers

Cook until soft, sieve and reheat. Add ½ cup sugar and ¼ cup salt. Bring to a boil and pour in sterilized jars and seal.

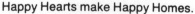

Happy Hearts make Happy Homes.

Cheeses, Dips, Soups and Sauces

A HANDY SPICE AND HERB GUIDE

ALLSPICE—a pea-sized fruit that grows in Mexico, Jamaica, Central and South America. Its delicate flavor resembles a blend of cloves, cinnamon and nutmeg. USES: (Whole) Pickles, meats, boiled fish, gravies. (Ground) Puddings, relishes, fruit preserves, baking.

BASIL—the dried leaves and stems of an herb grown in the United States and North Mediterranean area. Has an aromatic, leafy flavor. USES: For flavoring tomato dishes and tomato paste, turtle soup; also use in cooked peas, squash, snap beans; sprinkle chopped over lamb chops and poultry.

BAY LEAVES—the dried leaves of an evergreen grown in the eastern Mediterranean countries. Has a sweet, herbaceous floral spice note. USES: For pickling, stews, for spicing sauces and soup. Also use with a variety of meats and fish.

CARAWAY—the seed of a plant grown in the Netherlands. Flavor that combines the tastes of Anise and Dill. USES: For the cordial Kummel, baking breads; often added to sauerkraut, noodles, cheese spreads. Also adds zest to French fried potatoes, liver, canned asparagus.

CURRY POWDER—a ground blend of ginger, turmeric, fenugreek seed, as many as 16 to 20 spices. USES: For all Indian curry recipes such as lamb, chicken, and rice, eggs, vegetables, and curry puffs.

DILL—the small, dark seed of the dill plant grown in India, having a clean, aromatic taste. USES: Dill is a predominant seasoning in pickling recipes; also adds pleasing flavor to sauerkraut, potato salad, cooked macaroni, and green apple pie.

MACE—the dried covering around the nutmeg seed. Its flavor is similar to nutmeg, but with a fragrant, delicate difference. USES: (Whole) For pickling, fish, fish sauce, stewed fruit. (Ground) Delicious in baked goods, pastries and doughnuts, adds unusual flavor to chocolate desserts.

MARJORAM—an herb of the mint family, grown in France and Chile. Has a minty-sweet flavor. USES: In beverages, jellies and to flavor soups, stews, fish, sauces. Also excellent to sprinkle on lamb while roasting.

MSG (MONOSODIUM GLUTAMATE)—is a vegetable protein derivative for raising the effectiveness of natural food flavors. USES: Small amounts, adjusted to individual taste, can be added to steaks, roasts, chops, seafoods, stews, soups, chowder, chop suey and cooked vegetables.

OREGANO—a plant of the mint family and a species of marjoram of which the dried leaves are used to make an herb seasoning. USES: An excellent flavoring for any tomato dish, especially pizza, chili con carne, and Italian specialties.

PAPRIKA—a mild, sweet red pepper growing in Spain, Central Europe and the United States. Slightly aromatic and prized for brilliant red color. USES: A colorful garnish for pale foods, and for seasoning Chicken Paprika, Hungarian Goulash, salad dressings.

POPPY—the seed of a flower grown in Holland. Has a rich fragrance and crunchy, nut-like flavor. USES: Excellent as a topping for breads, rolls and cookies. Also delicious in buttered noodles.

ROSEMARY—an herb (like a curved pine needle) grown in France, Spain, and Portugal, and having a sweet, fresh taste. USES: In lamb dishes, in soups, stews and to sprinkle on beef before roasting.

SAGE—the leaf of a shrub grown in Greece, Yugoslavia and Albania. Flavor is camphoraceous and minty. USES: For meat and poultry stuffing, sausages, meat loaf, hamburgers, stews and salads.

THYME—the leaves and stems of a shrub grown in France and Spain. Has a strong, distinctive flavor. USES: For poultry seasoning, in croquettes, fricassees and fish dishes. Also tasty on fresh sliced tomatoes.

TURMERIC—a root of the ginger family, grown in India, Haiti, Jamaica and Peru, having a mild, ginger-pepper flavor. USES: As a flavoring and coloring in prepared mustard and in combination with mustard as a flavoring for meats, dressings, salads.

CHEESES, DIPS, SOUPS AND SAUCES

Seek first the Kingdom of God, and his righteousness; and all these things shall be added unto you. Matthew 6:33

ROYAL TOMATO SOUP

6 onions, chopped
1 bunch celery, chopped (use small
    fresh leaves)
8 qt. fresh tomatoes, cored but not
    peeled

1 c. sugar
¼ c. salt
1 c. oleo (room temperature)
1 c. flour

Place onions and celery in large pot with small amount of water just to keep from burning. Simmer while you fix tomatoes and add to pot. Cook, stirring as needed until vegetables are done. Put through food mill or ricer. Return pulp and juice to large kettle, add sugar and salt. Cream together butter and flour. When completely blended, add to the boiling hot pulp and juice. Stir well and continue simmering until slightly thick. Cook as you would if you were making gravy. Pour into sterile pint jars and seal immediately. Makes 10 to 11 pints.

JUDY'S CHEESE SAUSAGE BALLS

May be frozen. Great for parties!

1 lb. good brand sausage, cooked
    and drained

1 lb. shredded Cheddar cheese
3 c. Bisquick mix

Mix well. Shape into small balls. Put on a cookie sheet and bake for 15 to 20 minutes in 375° oven.

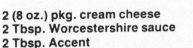

CHIPPED BEEF BALL

2 (8 oz.) pkg. cream cheese
2 Tbsp. Worcestershire sauce
2 Tbsp. Accent

1 pkg. chipped beef
4 whole green onions

Set cheese out ½ hour before making cheese ball. Chop onion and beef. Set ½ beef aside. Mix other ingredients and form ball. Roll ball in other half of beef. Refrigerate.

MILDRED'S CLAM CHOWDER

Your guests will rave! I, personally, have never tasted any better.

5 cans cream of potato soup
3 cans Campbell's clam chowder
3 cans minced clams

½ c. chopped celery &
1 medium onion, sauteed in 1 stick
    butter
2 qt. half & half

Mix well and bake 4 hours in 250 oven.
Note: 1 quart half & half & 1 quart of milk is fine to use in this recipe.

Those who bring sunshine into the lives of others, cannot keep it from themselves.

FESTIVE SPINACH DIP

1 pkg. frozen chopped spinach, well drained
1 c. sour cream
1 c. mayonnaise

½ c. chopped green onions
2 Tbsp. McCormick Salad Supreme
1 Tbsp. lemon juice

Mix well and chill.

MEXICAN LAYER DIP

1 can bean dip
2 mashed avocados, mixed with ½ c. mayonnaise
1 oz. sour cream with taco seasoning mix

½ lb. grated cheese
3 diced tomatoes
1 can ripe olives
Green onions, chopped

Layer in flat dish. Serve with tortilla chips.

SALMON LOG

1 can salmon
8 oz. cream cheese
2 Tbsp. grated onion

¼ tsp. horseradish
¼ tsp. salt
¼ tsp. liquid smoke

Mix and chill; roll in pecans and parsley.

DILL DIP
(It's a dilly!)

⅔ c. sour cream
1 c. mayonnaise
3 oz. cream cheese
1 Tbsp. dill weed
1 Tbsp. onion flakes

1 Tbsp. parsley flakes
1½ tsp. Beau Monde seasoning
1 Tbsp. Worcestershire sauce
Salt and pepper to taste
3 drops of Tabasco (optional)

Mix all ingredients together thoroughly. Refrigerate overnight. Serve with raw vegetables or crackers.

Note: A great dip for fresh vegetables.

Happiness in the Heart puts Sunshine in the day.

CREAMY CHEESE AND BACON SPREAD
(Brighten a brunch)

½ lb. sliced bacon, cooked and
    crumbled
8 oz. cream cheese, softened
¼ c. orange marmalade

Celery
Apple slices
Crackers

1. Combine bacon and cream cheese to marmalade.
2. Refrigerate mixture. Allow spread to reach room temperature at serving time.
3. Serve with celery sticks, apple slices and crackers.

ROYAL RAISIN SAUCE
(For meats)

A delicious sauce to serve on ham, ham loaf or roast pork!

Simmer 1 cup raisins in 2 cups water 15 minutes. Make paste of 2 tablespoons cornstarch, 2 tablespoons sugar, ⅛ teaspoon salt, and 2 tablespoons cold water. Add to raisins. Heat until thick. Remove from heat. Add 1 tablespoon butter or margarine and 2 tablespoons lemon juice. Mix well.

"A raisin is a grape that's had too many worries."

CHRISTMAS CONFETTI DIP

⅔ c. dairy sour cream
⅓ c. mayonnaise
2 Tbsp. choped onion

2 Tbsp. chopped chives
2 Tbsp. chopped pimento
¼ tsp. garlic powder

Mix all ingredients and chill.

CHEESE BALL

This is a fantastic cheese ball, with a distinctive flavor that everyone will love.

2 (8oz) pkg cream cheese,
    softened
1 small can crushed pineapple,
    drained

2 Tsp. dried onion flakes
⅓ c. chopped green pepper
2 Tsp. McCormick Salad Supreme
Chopped pecans

Mix the first 5 ingredients well and roll in chopped pecans. Chill and serve. Keeps well.

Celebrate each new day.

BEEF SANDWICH SPREAD
(Save and use those leftover bits of meat.)

2 c. finely chopped roast, beef steak
   and etc.
2 or 3 chopped hard-boiled eggs

3 Tbsp. sweet pickle relish
5 Tbsp. mayonnaise

Mix above with mayonnaise to desired consistency.

FRESH FRUIT DIP

1 (8 oz.) pkg. cream cheese,
   softened

1 (7 oz.) jar marshmallow creme
1 Tbsp. lemon juice

Combine cream cheese and marshmallow creme. Mix well. Serve with fresh fruit and cookies as dippers. Makes 2 cups. Strawberries, pear spears, orange sections, apples and bananas may be used.

You've got to do your own growing, no matter how tall your Grandfather was.

CHILI SAUCE

1 gal. tomatoes
3 to 4 green peppers
3 to 4 onions
1 red pepper
2 c. vinegar

3½ c. sugar
2 Tbsp. salt
1 tsp. cinnamon
Dash of black pepper

Bring tomatoes to a boil and skim liquid off the top. Add ingredients and cook till thick. Put in jars while hot and seal.

DONNA'S SALSA
(Delicious! Pass the sauce.)

½ tsp. garlic salt
1 qt. tomatoes, chopped fine
1 tsp. salt
2 tsp. sugar
1 tsp. oregano

1 onion, chopped
½ can green chiles, chopped or
   diced
1 Tbsp. oil
1 Tbsp. vinegar

Boil all together for 1 minute.

Note: Can be used as chip dip, as taco sauce or even scrambled eggs.

Happiness is not a destination, but a method of travel.

SWISS CHEESE SOUP

2 Tbsp. butter
3 Tbsp. flour
3 c. boiling water
1 pkg. dehydrated onion soup mix

2 c. milk
1½ c. shredded Swiss cheese (6 oz. pkg.)
Parsley

In medium size pan, melt butter. Stir in flour; cook over low heat till mixture bubbles and color starts to turn golden. Remove from heat. Pour in boiling water. Sprinkle onion soup mix on top; return to heat and cook for 15 minutes. Add milk and cheese. Heat just till cheese starts to melt. Garnish with parsley.

GREEN CHILIE DIP
(Serve with corn chips or crackers)

2 Tbsp. butter or margarine
1 (4 oz.) can chopped green chilies
½ c. chopped onion

1 c. tomatoes, strained
1 lb. Velveeta cheese
Salt to taste

Saute onion in butter until tender. Add tomatoes, chilies and salt. Simmer 19 minutes. Remove from heat, add cheese, chopped.

BROCCOLI SOUP

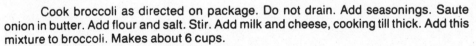

10 oz. frozen chopped broccoli
Salt and pepper
¼ c. grated onion
4 Tbsp. butter

4 Tbsp. flour
1 qt. milk
1 c. grated cheese

Cook broccoli as directed on package. Do not drain. Add seasonings. Saute onion in butter. Add flour and salt. Stir. Add milk and cheese, cooking till thick. Add this mixture to broccoli. Makes about 6 cups.

For an attractive serving trick, place bits of cheese or fruit on picks.

One teaspoon of vinegar added to the water in which eggs are poached keeps the whites from spreading and makes the whites cook over yolk.

The journey of a thousand miles begins with one step.
When love and skill work together, expect a masterpiece.

❤ Notes

Salads

EQUIVALENT CHART

3 tsp.	1 tbsp.	¼ lb. crumbled Bleu cheese	1 c.
2 tbsp.	⅛ c.	1 lemon	3 tbsp. juice
4 tbsp.	¼ c.	1 orange	⅓ c. juice
8 tbsp.	½ c.	1 lb. unshelled walnuts	1½ to 1¾ c. shelled
16 tbsp.	1 c.	2 c. fat	1 lb.
5 tbsp. + 1 tsp.	⅓ c.	1 lb. butter	2 c. or 4 sticks
12 tbsp.	¾ c.	2 c. granulated sugar	1 lb.
4 oz.	½ c.	3½ - 4 c. unsifted powdered sugar	1 lb.
8 oz.	1 c.	2¼ c. packed brown sugar	1 lb.
16 oz.	1 lb.	4 c. sifted flour	1 lb.
1 oz.	2 tbsp. fat or liquid	4½ c. cake flour	1 lb.
2 c.	1 pt.	3½ c. unsifted whole wheat flour	1 lb.
2 pt.	1 qt.	4 oz. (1 to 1¼ c.) uncooked	
1 qt.	4 c.	macaroni	2¼ c. cooked
⅝ c.	½ c. + 2 tbsp.	7 oz. spaghetti	4 c. cooked
⅞ c.	¾ c. + 2 tbsp.	4 oz. (1½ to 2 c.) uncooked	
1 jigger	1½ fl. oz. (3 tbsp.)	noodles	2 c. cooked
8 to 10 egg whites	1 c.	28 saltine crackers	1 c. crumbs
12 to 14 egg yolks	1 c.	4 slices bread	1 c. crumbs
1 c. unwhipped cream	2 c. whipped	14 square graham crackers	1 c. crumbs
1 lb. shredded American cheese	4 c.	22 vanilla wafers	1 c. crumbs

SUBSTITUTIONS FOR A MISSING INGREDIENT

1 square **chocolate** (1 ounce) = 3 or 4 tablespoons cocoa plus ½ tablespoon fat.
1 tablespoon **cornstarch** (for thickening) = 2 tablespoons flour.
1 cup sifted **all-purpose flour** = 1 cup plus 2 tablespoons sifted cake flour.
1 cup sifted **cake flour** = 1 cup minus 2 tablespoons sifted all-purpose flour.
1 teaspoon **baking powder** = ¼ teaspoon baking soda plus ½ teaspoon cream of tartar.
1 cup **sour milk** = 1 cup sweet milk into which 1 tablespoon vinegar or lemon juice has been
    stirred; or 1 cup buttermilk (let stand for 5 minutes).
1 cup **sweet milk** = 1 cup sour milk or buttermilk plus ½ teaspoon baking soda.
¾ cup **cracker crumbs** = 1 cup bread crumbs.
1 cup **cream, sour, heavy** = ⅓ cup butter and ⅔ cup milk in any sour milk recipe.
1 teaspoon **dried herbs** = 1 tablespoon fresh herbs.
1 cup **whole milk** = ½ cup evaporated milk and ½ cup water or 1 cup reconstituted nonfat dry
    milk and 1 tablespoon butter.
1 package **active dry yeast** = 1 cake compressed yeast.
1 tablespoon **instant minced onion, rehydrated** = 1 small fresh onion.
1 tablespoon **prepared mustard** = 1 teaspoon dry mustard.
⅛ teaspoon **garlic powder** = 1 small pressed clove of garlic.
1 lb. **whole dates** = 1½ c. pitted and cut.
3 medium **bananas** = 1 c. mashed.
3 c. **dry corn flakes** = 1 c. crushed.
10 **miniature marshmallows** = 1 large marshmallow.

GENERAL OVEN CHART

Very slow oven	250° to 300° F.
Slow oven	300° to 325° F.
Moderate oven	325° to 375° F.
Medium hot oven	375° to 400° F.
Hot oven	400° to 450° F.
Very hot oven	450° to 500° F.

CONTENTS OF CANS

Of the different sizes of cans used by commercial canners, the most common are:

Size:	Average Contents
8-oz.	1 cup
picnic	1¼ cups
No. 300	1¾ cups
No. 1 tall	2 cups
No. 303	2 cups
No. 2	2½ cups
No. 2½	3½ cups
No. 3	4 cups
No. 10	12 to 13 cups

SALADS

(Husband) "What did you do all day?"
I didn't wash the dishes,
And I didn't make the bed,
Your clothes are
Where you left them--
I sat all day and read.
I overlooked the ironing,
The wash and mending too,
As far as I'm concerned
There's not a thing to do.
Your supper isn't ready
And the toys are in the way
And that, my darling husband,
Is what I didn't do
All day.

ORANGE FLUFF SALAD

A salad you can put together in a few minutes. Take my word for it, you'll enjoy the refreshing flavor!

1 (8 oz.) ctn. whipped topping
1 (3 oz.) pkg. orange Jello
1 (8 oz.) can crushed pineapple, drained

1 small can mandarin oranges, drained
1 small ctn. cottage cheese

Put whipped topping into large bowl. Sprinkle with Jello. Stir well and add balance of ingredients. Refrigerate.

Note: Can be served on shredded lettuce.

For a variety, substitute cherry Jello and a can of drained dark Bing cherries, For the Orange Jello add Mandarian Oranges.

GARDEN VEGETABLE SALAD

I took this dish to a sports banquet, introducing it to people who wanted the recipe. It disappeared fast!

1 head cauliflower
2 to 3 bunches green onions
3 stalks broccoli
1 bunch radishes

1 pkg. original Hidden Valley Ranch
1 c. mayonnaise
1 c. sour cream or 1 c. plain yogurt

Cut vegetables in bite-size pieces. Mix mayonnaise, sour cream and Hidden Valley Ranch together in small bowl and add to the vegetables. Mix well.

Hint: This will keep for 2 days refrigerated.

"One of the most attractive things you can wear is a smile."

21

"Make prayer a top priority rather than a last resort."

RIBBON JELLO SALAD

My niece Jan Farris, really made a hit at a holiday dinner with her colorful layered salad. A delightful salad to impress your guests.

2 pkg. Knox gelatine
½ c. water
2 c. milk
2 c. sour cream
1½ c. sugar
2 tsp. vanilla

1 (3 oz.) pkg. orange gelatin
1 (3 oz.) pkg. lime gelatin
1 (3 oz.) pkg. blackberry gelatin (or any dark gelatin)
1 (3 oz.) pkg. lemon gelatin
1 (3 oz.) pkg. cherry gelatin

White filling: Mix Knox gelatine in water and add milk. Bring almost to a boil. Beat until creamy the sour cream, sugar and vanilla. Add to gelatin mixture and mix well. Divide into three equal parts.

Gelatin layers: Dissolve orange flavored gelatin with 1½ cups hot water and cool slightly. Layer in an attractive clear bowl like this: Orange Jello, white filling, then let orange gelatin set before adding white filling again. Next is the lime gelatin, let set, then add white filling. Next the blackberry or any dark gelatin, let set. Then add white filling. Next the lemon gelatin, let set and add white filling. Last, add the cherry gelatin and let set.

MARGIE'S RED RASPBERRY SALAD
(Delicious!!)

1 pkg. raspberry salad
1 (8 oz.) pkg. cream cheese
1 (8 oz.) pkg. frozen red raspberries
1 small can crushed pineapple, drained

½ c. chopped nuts
1 (8 oz.) container whipped topping

Fix raspberry Jello, using 1 cup hot water and juice drained from raspberries plus enough water to make 1 cup. Beat cream cheese into hot Jello with mixer. Chill till like thick syrup. Beat again and beat in the whipped topping. Fold in drained pineapple, raspberries and nuts. Add 1 sliced banana if desired. Chill.

MA'S CRANBERRY SALAD
(Delicious! Serve in crystal bowl.)

1 pkg. raw cranberries, ground
1 small pkg. strawberry Jello
2 c. sugar

1 c. nuts, chopped or 2 apples, chopped or ground, or 2 oranges, chopped or ground

Mix Jello with 1¾ cups water. When about congealed, add rest of ingredients and mix well. Set in refrigerator to jell.

Kindness is the language the deaf can hear and the blind can see.

MEXICALI TACO SALAD

1 lb. hamburger
1 chopped onion
1 can pitted ripe olives (optional)
1 can red kidney beans
3 tomatoes, chopped
1 head lettuce
¼ c. green pepper, chopped
    (optional)

1 small bottle Thousand Island
    dressing
4 oz. shredded Cheddar cheese
1 pkg. Doritos tortilla chips (taco
    flavored), crushed
½ c. taco sauce

Brown hamburger and add onion, olives and beans. Season hamburger with taco sauce, add other ingredients and mix in a large bowl just before serving.

FROZEN FRUIT SALAD
(Eye catching, easy and so good.)

Boil:

1 c. sugar

1 c. juice from apricots

Cool.

Add:

1 box frozen strawberries
1 c. crushed pineapple and juice
1 c. apricots, cut in quarters

4 bananas, sliced and quartered
2 or 3 peaches, diced

Mix together and freeze in small serving containers.

CHERLYN'S PEACH SALAD
(A Delicious Summer Salad)

2 pkg. peach Jello (gel as
    directed on package)
1¼ c. Cool Whip

4 c. sliced fresh peaches
1 - 1½ c. white seedless grapes

Beat the whip cream into the Jello that has set. Add peaches and grapes.

CHRISTMAS SALAD

A pretty salad for the holidays, my sister Shirley Jean shared this good recipe with me.

2 pkg. lime Jello
2 pkg. cherry or strawberry Jello
8 oz. pkg. cream cheese
1 c. miniature marshmellows

½ c. finely chopped nuts
1 medium can crushed pineapple, drained
½ pt. whipping cream, whipped

Mix lime Jello with 3 cups boiling water. Add marshmallows and cream cheese. If it all doesn't dissolve, strain it. Set in refrigerator until starts to set. Mix drained pineapple with whipped cream and nuts for the second layer. Mix red Jello, using the normal amount of water called for on package. Let almost jell and put on top layer. Add a dab of Cool Whip if desired when serving.

Note: Use 9x13 inch pan. Makes 12 servings.

It matters not
If it's red, green or yellow.
There's nothing you can disguise
Like a bowl full of Jello.

PEACH-PINEAPPLE SALAD

A tasty recipe, from our daughter-in-law Patty, who puts a jest into cooking.

1 large can peaches, drained
1 large can crushed pineapple, drained
4 Tbsp. ReaLemon

1 can Eagle Brand milk
1 c. chopped nuts
1 (8 oz.) ctn. Cool Whip

Mash peaches; add other ingredients, stirring in the Cool Whip last.

CHERRY COKE SALAD

2 boxes cherry Jello
12 oz. bottle Coke
1 c. pecans

Large can crushed pineapple
1 can dark sweet pitted cherries
8 oz. cream cheese

Drain cherries and pineapple. Heat juice and pour over Jello. Dissolve and let cool. Add Coke; chill until syrupy. Add cream cheese, cut into tiny pieces; add fruits and nuts. Chill.

LIME SALAD

Delicious. Can be used in a mold

1 pkg. Lime Gelatin
1 ¼ c. boiling water
1 ½ c. miniature marshmellows
½ c. whipping cream or
8 oz. carton cool whip

2 small cans crushed pineapple with juice
1 c. cottage cheese
½ c. nuts

Dissolve gelatin in water and add marshmellows. Add pinneapple with juice. Add cottage cheese, nuts and whipped cream. Chill and serve.

CARROT SALAD

When I see a salad with fresh shredded carrots, I am reminded of a friend Joe Williams, who was a dedicated Air Force pilot. He faithfully had carrots in his diet almost daily, convincing me that carrots are very good for one's eyes. Sometimes he would just eat the combination of raisins and shredded carrots.

3 c. shredded carrots
1 (15½ oz.) can pineapple chunks or
    tidbits, drained
⅔ c. salad dressing

½ c. raisins
½ c. celery, chopped
Lettuce leaves

Combine all ingredients except lettuce; mix lightly. Chill. Serve salad in lettuce lined bowl.

LEMON JELLO DELIGHT SALAD

Served cut in squares and put on a lettuce leaf or just spoon from a bowl. You will be glad to have this recipe.

1 box lemon Jello
1 c. miniature marshmallows
1 c. crushed pineapple, drained well
3 sliced bananas

1 egg
2 Tbsp. flour
½ c. sugar
Whipped topping

Mix Jello according to directions. Add to hot Jello the marshmallows and pineapple. Cool and add bananas and let set. Cook until thick, the juice from pineapple, adding water to make 1 cup, the beaten egg, sugar and flour. Cool and pour over first layer. Cover with with whipped topping. Sprinkle with nuts if desired.

SEVEN LAYERED SALAD
(This is great prepared ahead of time)

1 head lettuce
1 c. celery, diced
⅓ c. onion, diced
1 tomato, diced
1 (10 oz.) pkg. frozen peas

Real bacon bits
6 oz. grated Cheddar cheese
2 c. mayonnaise
2 Tbsp. sugar

Cut lettuce in bite-size pieces. Place on bottom of airtight container. Layer remaining items on top. Add mayonnaise and sugar; spread over vegetables, as you would ice a cake. Top with grated cheese. Cover and refrigerate.

Crisp fresh vegetables are everyone's delight,
Buy them in season, the price will be right.
Cook, fry or toss for a salad,
Vegetables always are a pleasing sight.

More things are wrought through prayer than this world dreams of.

UNUSUAL SALAD

21 oz. can cherry pie filling
1 (No. 2) can crushed pineapple (not
   drained)

1 (8 oz.) ctn. Cool Whip
1 can Eagle Brand milk
½ c. nuts (optional)

Mix all ingredients together, chill and serve.

COTTAGE CHEESE SALAD
(Delicious!)

1 pkg. lemon Jello
1 lb. small curd cottage cheese
1 c. whipped cream
1 c. boiling water

1 small can crushed pineapple,
   drained
1 small bottle maraschino cherries

Dissolve Jello in boiling water. Let stand until like thick syrup. Add cottage cheese and pineapple. Fold in whipped cream and cherries. A few nuts may be added if desired. Pour into molds and set until firm.

RECIPE FOR HAPPINESS

Take:

2 heaping cups of patience
1 heartful of love

2 handsful of generosity
1 headful of understanding

Sprinkle generously with kindness. add plenty of faith, mix well and spread over a lifetime and serve everyone you meet!

POTATO SALAD

My favorite potato salad, I think of it as the old fashioned kind. A delicious recipe from our sister-in-law Fran Remole, of Potomac, Il., this always wins approval of family and friends!

6 large potatoes, boiled and diced
4 hard-boiled eggs, diced
½ c. chopped green pepper
¼ c. chopped onion
½ c. sweet relish
¼ tsp. celery seed

Salt and pepper to taste
1 c. salad dressing
1 tsp. mustard (or more, optional)
2 Tbsp. sugar
¼ c. milk

Prepare all ingredients except dressing. Mix salad dressing, mustard, sugar and milk and mix into other. Taste, if not enough dressing, prepare and add more.

Happiness is like potato salad
When you share it with others, it's a picnic.

CELERY SEED SALAD DRESSING

This is very much like the "House" dressing in some restaurants.

¾ c. vinegar
⅛ c. water
1 egg
2 tsp. salt
1 c. sugar

1 tsp. powdered mustard
1 to 2 tsp. grated onion
2 c. salad oil
1 Tbsp. celery seed

Mix ingredients in electric mixer on high speed for 20 minutes. In a blender, use medium speed about 15 seconds. (No need to grate onion if using blender.)

Every little vegetable has a flavor of its own
And all these tasty vegetables
Will win themselves a home.

KOREAN SALAD

This makes a big salad. Great for a luncheon, or store part of it without the dressing. "You'll be impressed."

1 lb. fresh spinach, drained well to
   prevent weeping
1 small head lettuce
1 (5 oz.) can water chestnuts,
   drained and sliced

1 lb. can bean sprouts, drained
4 hard cooked eggs, chopped
¾ lb. bacon, fried, drained and
   crumbled (or use real bacon
   bits)

Wash spinach, trim and drain thoroughly. Tear the lettuce and mix with the other ingredients. Mix the dressing ingredients in the blender.

KOREAN SALAD DRESSING

¼ c. sugar
⅓ c. catsup
¼ c. vinegar
2 t. worcestershire sauce

1 medium onion, grated
salt to taste
1 c. salad oil

Combine dressing ingredients, adding oil last.

ORANGE DELIGHT SALAD

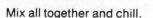

1 pkg. orange gelatin
1 pkg. vanilla pudding (not instant)

3 c. water

Cook the above till it thickens and let it cool.

Then add:

1 medium box refrigerated whipped
   topping
1 can crushed pineapple, drained

1 c. mandarin oranges, drained
1 jar maraschino cherries, drained
   and cut up

Mix all together and chill.

POPPY SEED DRESSING

⅔ c. sugar
1 tsp. dry mustard
1 tsp. salt
1 c. cooking oil

⅓ c. white vinegar
1 Tbsp. grated onion
2 tsp. poppy seed
1½ tsp. lemon juice

Mix dry ingredients. Add vinegar, add oil slowly while beating with electric mixer until thick. Add lemon juice and poppy seed. Store in refrigerator. Set out 2 hours before pouring over broccoli, cauliflower, celery and mushrooms.

STRAWBERRY SALAD

This was originally my mother's recipe, a family tradition. It is a pretty salad, nice for the holidays, served in a pretty dish.

2 pkg. strawberry Jello
2 boxes frozen strawberries
1 can crushed pineapple
2 bananas, mashed

1½ c. boiling water
1 c. sour cream
½ c. chopped nuts (optional)

Dissolve Jello in boiling water; add strawberries, drained pineapple, mashed bananas and nuts. Pour ½ mixture in separate bowls. Let set until firm. Spread sour cream on top, then add rest of mixture.

Note: Eight ounces cream cheese mixed with the sour cream is optional.

BANANA SALAD

A different, but delicious dish! Serve with meal, but would be good over ice cream too.

1 c. light brown sugar
1 Heaping Tbsp. flour

1 c. cream
¾ c. nuts, broken in pieces

Mix brown sugar, flour and cream together and cook over medium heat until mixture boils, thickens and cooks down some, approximately 3 or 4 minutes. Remove from heat and beat with spoon until cream consistency. Cool. Add nuts. Pour over bananas which have been peeled, cut into halves and placed in serving bowl.

"If it ever happens that some people should be to tired to give you a smile, why not leave one of yours?" For nobody needs a smile so much as one who has no smile to give.

♡ CRANBERRY SALAD

2 c. cranberries
1 c. water
1 c. sugar
1 pkg. red jello

1 c. chopped apples
1 c. drained crushed
  pineapple
1 c. diced celery
1 c. chopped nuts

Combine water, sugar and cranberries and boil until all berries burst their jackets. Pour over the package of jello and allow to cool; then add apples, nuts and celery. Set before serving.

MISSISSIPPI SUNSHINE FRUIT SALAD

What a delightful salad and the recipe from my Aunt Bernice in Mississippi. Have you heard of bananas not turning dark in color setting overnight? Attractive and can be an overnight salad. The bananas stay shiny and is a colorful, refreshing salad, again I've found pleasure in sharing another recipe!

1 (20 oz.) can pineapple
1 Tbsp. lemon juice
1 Tbsp. orange peel
⅓ c. orange juice
11 oz. can mandarin oranges,
    drained

2 unpeeled apples, diced
2 sliced bananas
½ c. sugar
2 Tbsp. cornstarch

Mix sugar and cornstarch. Blend in lemon juice, orange and orange peel and ¾ cup pineapple juice. Bring to a boil. Boil 1 minute stirring constantly. Pour hot mixture over fruit. Refrigerate overnight *uncovered.* Will keep very well.

Note: Put salad in a pretty clear salad bowl, and remember, uncovered.

RASPBERRY SALAD
(Especially good with ham)

2 pkg. red raspberry gelatin
1½ c. applesauce
2⅔ c. hot water

1 (8 oz.) pkg. frozen raspberries
Chopped nuts

Dressing:

2 c. small marshmallows

½ pt. sour cream

Dissolve gelatin in hot water, then stir in ingredients. Dressing is made by adding 2 cups small marshmallows to ½ pint sour cream. Let set overnight then beat well. Spread over top of gelatin salad.

HOT CHICKEN SALAD
(Great for a Luncheon)

2 c. chopped cooked chicken
1 ½ c. diced celery
½ c. slivered almonds
½ t. salt
2 t. grated onion

1 T. lemon juice
1 c. mayonnaise
½ c. shredded cheddar
    cheese
1 c. crushed potato
    chips

Combine first 7 ingredients. Toss until well mixed. Pile lightly into greased baking dish. Sprinkle with shredded Cheddar cheese and crushed potato chips. Bake at 375 for 20 minutes. Serve hot.

The fruit of the spirit is love.
Joy, peace, longsuffering
Gentleness, goodness, faith,
Meekness, temperance. Galatians 22-23

APRICOT SALAD SURPREME

2 pkg. peach gelatin
2 c. boiling water
1 c. miniature marshmallows

1 (No. 2½) can apricots
1 (No. 2) can crushed pineapple

Topping:

1 c. pineapple juice
1 egg
2 c. sugar
3 Tbsp. flour

2 Tbsp. butter
Whipped topping
½ c. chopped walnuts or grated
    Cheddar cheese (optional)

Dissolve gelatin and marshmallows in boiling water in a 9½ x 13 inch baking dish. Drain juice from apricots, adding enough water to make 2 cups. Add this to above mixture and chill till "shaky." Drain pineapple and reserve juice for topping. Add diced apricots and pineapple to gelatin and chill till firm.

Topping: Combine sugar and flour and blend into beaten egg in small saucepan. Gradually stir in pineapple juice (add water to equal 1 cup if needed). Cook over medium heat till thick, stirring constantly. Remove from heat and stir in butter and cool. Fold in 2 cups whipped topping. Fold in cooled dressing and spread over gelatin. Sprinkle generously with chopped walnuts or grated Cheddar cheese. Chill.

"This can be used as a dessert salad, served with nut bread."

GLORIFIED RICE

This a special dish to me, because I remember my grandmother making it when I was a young girl. Delicious.

1 pkg. lemon Jello
1 c. boiling water
1 c. cooked rice
½ c. nutmeats

Small can crushed pineapple
¾ c. marshmallows
½ c. powdered sugar
1 c. whipping cream

Dissolve Jello in boiling water. Cool. When mixture starts to congeal, add rice mixed with sugar, nuts, pineapple and marshmallows. Fold in beaten whipped cream.

Grandma was a special person to me,
All you would think a Grandmother would be,
She taught me how to cook, you see.
As she laughed and instructed me,
I wonder at times how she did endure,
She was a genuine Grandma, that is for sure.

30

SHELL MACARONI TUNA SALAD

A recipe from my friend and birthday twin Norma Parrett, from Moberly, Mo., this is a super warm weather dish you are sure to enjoy.

1 pkg. shell macaroni
1 (7 oz.) can tuna
2 Tbsp. chopped onion
½ c. cooked peas

½ c. chopped green pepper
¼ c. sliced olives
1 Tbsp. chopped pimento
½ c. mayonnaise

Cook macaroni in 2 quarts of boiling, salted water for about 10 minutes. Drain and rinse in cold water. Drain well. Add ingredients and chill. Serve on tomato slice or lettuce.

Ideas are funny little things;
They don't work unless you do.

PISTACHIO PUDDING

Good served as a salad or a dessert. Maraschino cherries cut in halves and placed 2½ inches apart over the top is attractive.

1 (3½ oz.) pkg. instant pistachio
   pudding mix
1 (13½ oz.) ctn. frozen whipped
   topping
1 (8¼ oz.) can crushed pineapple
1 (11 oz.) can mandarin oranges,
   drained

1 c. miniature marshmallows
1 (12 oz.) ctn. small curd cottage
   cheese (optional)
⅓ c. chopped pecans (optional)
Maraschino cherries (optional)

Be kindly affectioned one to another with brotherly love ... given to hospitality (Romans 12:10, 13)

WARM PINEAPPLE SALAD

"This is so good served with ham or a quick salad to take to a Pot Luck."

1 (No. 2) can pineapple chunks or
   tidbits, drained (save juice)
2 eggs, well beaten
2 c. yellow mild cheese, cubed

½ c. sugar
1 Tbsp. flour
1 c. reserved pineapple juice

Combine pineapple juice, flour and 3 beaten eggs and cook until thick. Add pineapple chunks and cubed cheese. Serve immediately while warm or serve cooled.

Ask, and it shall be given you;
Seek and you shall find;
Knock, and it shall be opened to you. (Matthew 7:7)

31

CRANBERRIES WITH MARSHMALLOWS
(Delicious if you like cranberries!)

1 lb. cranberries
½ lb. miniature marshmallows

2 c. sugar
1 c. whipping cream

Chop cranberries with food chopper or in food processor. Add marshmallows and sugar. Whip cream and add it to other ingredients. Stir. Refrigerate overnight.

LUNCHEON CHICKEN SALAD
(A good choice for a Ladies Luncheon or Brunch)

Dark and light boned chicken, cut in
   cubes
Can chunk pineapple, drained
Can black olives
Jar green salad olives
Salt and pepper to taste

Slivered almonds
Mayonnaise
Pineapple juice
½ tsp. Dijon mustard (optional)
⅓ c. whipped topping (optional)

Mix the first 5 ingredients together with mayonnaise and some of the pineapple juice. Chill in refrigerator. Just before serving, add slivered almonds.

Note: If using Dijon mustard and whipped cream, mix with mayonnaise and pineapple juice.

Be kind and generous to those who are old,
For kindness is dearer and better than gold!

OLD FASHIONED COUNTRY BEAN SALAD

Quick to put together, chill well before serving. Always good.

1 (No. 2) can kidney beans
2 boiled eggs
⅓ c. chopped pickle or pickle relish
2 Tbsp. chopped onion

Salt and pepper to taste
½ tsp. celery seed
⅓ c. mayonnaise

INSTRUCTIONS FOR A FOOL-PROOF METHOD FOR BOILING EGGS:
WORKS PERFECTLY

1. Cover eggs with cold water in pan.
2. Bring to boil on high heat.
3. *Immediately!!!* turn off heat, leaving pan on burner, covering with lid that fits.
4. Let eggs "steam" 15 minutes.
5. Pour off hot water, rinse with cold.
6. Gently roll on counter and peel.

Use greased muffin tins as molds when baking stuffed green peppers.

To peel an orange easily and to get the skin off in one piece, heat the orange slightly for 3 to 4 minutes before peeling.

Heat lemons well before using and there will be more quantity of juice.

Green pepper is an excellent source of vitamin C. Cut in strips to serve as nibblers, add it to salads and sandwich fillings or blanch whole peppers and fill with tuna-potato salad.

Add 1 tablespoon minced onion, dehydrated, to replace 1 fresh onion.

Cast all your care upon him; for he careth for you. Peter 5:7

APPLE SALAD DRESSING

1 c. sugar
2 Tbsp. flour
1 c. water

Butter (size of hickory nut)
1 egg, beaten
3 Tbsp. vinegar

Mix well and boil until thickens, stirring constantly. Cool. Keeps well in covered container in refrigerator.

SURPRISE VEGTABLE SALAD

A bit different. The blend with cottage cheese makes this salad special. Make it the day before serving. Surprisingly good.

1 lb. cottage cheese
Scant ½ cup miracle whip
2 Tbsp. sugar, salt and pepper

1 tomato, chopped
1 onion, chopped
1 green pepper, chopped

Let set overnight.

All things work together for good to them that love God. (Romans 8:28)

ORIENTAL STYLE SALAD

Drain:

17 oz. can tiny peas
16 oz. can bean sprouts
12 oz. can whole grain corn
2 (5 oz.) cans water chestnuts,
    sliced

1 (6 oz.) can mushrooms, sliced
1 (4 oz.) can pimentos, cut up

Add:

1 green pepper, thinly sliced
1 large onion, thinly sliced

1 c. chopped celery

Combine in large bowl and pour dressing over. Refrigerate for 24 hours.

Dressing:

1 c. salad oil
1 c. water
1 c. sugar

¾ c. vinegar
Salt and pepper

****

We may not always realize
that everyhing we do
affect not only our lives,
but touches others too --

A Single Happy Smile
can always brighten up the day
For anyone who happens to be passing
your way.

And a liitle bit of Thoughtfulness
that shows Someone you care --
Creates a ray of Sunshine
for both of you to share

Yes, every time you offer Someone
a helping hand,
every time you show a friend
you care and understand,
Every time you have a kind and gentle word
to give,
You help Someone find beauty
in this precious life we live.

For Happiness brings Happiness,
and loving ways brings Love
And giving is the treasure
That Contentment is made of.

Vegetables, Casseroles, and Meats

MEAT ROASTING GUIDE

Cut	Weight Pounds	Approx. Time (Hours) (325° oven)	Internal Temperature
BEEF			
Standing Rib Roast [1]			
(10 inch) ribs)	4	1¾	140° (rare)
If using shorter cut (8-inch)		2	160° (medium)
ribs, allow 30 min. longer		2½	170° (well done)
	8	2½	140° (rare)
		3	160° (medium)
		4½	170° (well done)
Rolled Ribs	4	2	140° (rare)
		2½	160° (medium)
		3	170° (well done)
	6	3	140° (rare)
		3¼	160° (medium)
		4	170° (well done)
Rolled rump [2]	5	2¼	140° (rare)
		3	160° (medium)
		3¼	170° (well done)
Sirloin tip [2]	3	1½	140° (rare)
[2] Roast only if high quality.		2	160° (medium)
Otherwise, braise.		2¼	170° (well done)
LAMB			
Leg	6	3	175° (medium)
		3½	180° (well done)
	8	4	175° (medium)
		4½	180° (well done)
VEAL			
Leg (piece)	5	2½ to 3	170° (well done)
Shoulder	6	3½	170° (well done)
Rolled Shoulder	3 to 5	3 to 3½	170° (well done)

POULTRY ROASTING GUIDE

Type of Poultry	Ready-To-Cook Weight	Oven Temperature	Approx. Total Roasting Time
TURKEY	6 to 8 lbs.	325°	2½ to 3 hrs.
	8 to 12 lbs.	325°	3 to 3½ hrs.
	12 to 16 lbs.	325°	3½ to 4 hrs.
	16 to 20 lbs.	325°	4 to 4½ hrs.
	20 to 24 lbs.	300°	5 to 6 hrs.
CHICKEN	2 to 2½ lbs.	400°	1 to 1½ hrs.
(Unstuffed)	2½ to 4 lbs.	400°	1½ to 2½ hrs.
	4 to 8 lbs.	325°	3 to 5 hrs.
DUCK	3 to 5 lbs.	325°	2½ to 3 hrs.
(Unstuffed)			

NOTE: Small chickens are roasted at 400° so that they brown well in the short cooking time. They may also be done at 325° but will take longer and will not be as brown. Increase cooking time 15 to 20 minutes for stuffed chicken and duck.

VEGETABLES, CASSEROLES AND MEATS

If there's not enough left to save
And a little too much to dump
And there's nothing to do but eat it,
That could make the housewife plump!

Today well lived, makes every yesterday
A dream of happiness and every tomorrow
A vision of hope.

When boiling onions whole for stews, etc., before putting them into the liquid, stick a fork into them in several places, and no matter how large they are, they will cook.

An onion can make people cry,
But there is yet to be invented a
Vegetable that can make them laugh.

SAUSAGE AND EGGS CASSEROLE

12 slices white bread (crusts removed)
1 c. shredded cheese
2 c. cooked sausage (about 1½ lb.)
8 slightly beaten eggs

3½ c. milk
½ tsp. dry mustard
½ tsp. salt
Onion powder

Grease dish. Cut out doughnut from each slice of bread and fit scraps in bottom of dish. Sprinkle cheese over bread, add sausage and onion powder and place doughnuts on top. Combine eggs, milk, mustard and salt and pour over all. Cover and refrigerate at least six hours. Bake, uncovered, at 325° for 1 hour. Let set about 10 minutes before serving.

The mintage of wisdom is to know that rest is rust and that real life is love,

laughter, and work.

SARAH'S POTATO TOPPED CASSEROLE

Jeff and Jennifer's favorite casserole - and so easy!

1½ lb. ground chuck
1 each medium onion, chopped
Salt and pepper to taste

1 can whole kernel corn, drained
Mashed potatoes

Brown ground chuck and onion together in skillet until onion is transparent and meat is done. Drain well. Place meat and onion mixture in ungreased casserole. Layer the drained corn on top of meat mixture. Spread mashed potatoes over top of corn sealing edges and completely covering the corn. (You may use leftover mashed potatoes, instant mashed potatoes, or fresh mashed potatoes.) Bake in 350° oven for 30 minutes or until casserole is hot and potato peaks begin to brown. This casserole may be prepared ahead and frozen.

CAROL'S BRUNCH CASSEROLE

From my friend, Carol Kent who lives in Columbia, Missouri, a true gourmet cook! A great Christmas morning breakfast.

Use 16 slices white bread, crusts removed.

Place on each slice:

1 slice Canadian bacon, sliced thin
1 slice sharp Cheddar cheese

1 slice bread on top

Mix the following:

6 eggs, beaten
½ tsp. salt
¼ green pepper, chopped fine
½ tsp. Worcestershire sauce

3 c. whole milk
Dash of red pepper
½ tsp. dry mustard
¼ c. minced onion

Pour over the above and let stand overnight. Melt ½ cup butter and pour over top and then cover with 1 cup crushed potato chips. Bake 1 hour at 350°

FLUFFY EGGS AND BACON

½ lb. bacon (12 slices)
1 c. chopped onion
½ c. Bisquick mix
3 eggs
¼ c. milk

½ tsp. salt
¼ tsp. pepper
½ c. shredded Cheddar or Swiss
    cheese

Preheat oven. Grease 1½ quart round casserole. Cut bacon slices into thirds. Cook and stir bacon until almost crisp, add onion, cook and stir until bacon is crisp. Drain, spread bacon and onion in bottom of casserole. Beat Bisquick, eggs, milk, salt and pepper with hand beater until almost smooth. Slowly pour egg mixture over bacon, sprinkle with cheese. Bake until knife inserted comes out clean. Bake in 375° oven for 35 minutes.

Note: Ham may be substituted for bacon.

A good rule for talking is one used in measuring flour; sift first.

BREAKFAST CASSEROLE

12 sausage links
12 slices sandwich bread, crusts
    removed
¾ lb. grated Cheddar cheese

8 eggs
2½ c. milk
1 can mushroom soup

Break bread into cubes and place in 9x13 inch pan. Cut up sausage links. Add to cubed bread. Break eggs into milk and beat. Stir in soup with fork and place on top. With fork, lightly stir in cheese. Cook, uncovered, for 45 minutes in 350° oven. Serves 8.

EGG AND SAUSAGE CASSEROLE
(Can use ham)

When you plan to have a brunch for the "bunch" try this casserole. It will be enjoyed and can be frozen ahead of time.

1½ lb. sausage
8 slices sandwich bread
¾ lb. Cheddar cheese
4 eggs

2½ c. milk
¾ Tbsp. dry mustard
8 oz. can mushrooms
1 (10½ oz.) can mushroom soup

1. Brown sausage and drain.
2. Line 9x13 inch pan with cubed bread.
3. Layer pan with bread, sausage and cheese.
4. Beat egg with milk and mustard and pour over layers.
5. Cover and refrigerate overnight.
6. Remove for 1 hour at room temperature the next day.
7. Dilute soup with ½ cup milk, add mushrooms and add to the above.
Bake uncovered at 325° for 1 hour, or until firm.

BAKED BEANS

So easy, this quick recipe is so simple, yet has received numerous compliments. Goes well at a pot luck dinner, cook out or just a home meal. Always a favorite of our six sons.

31 oz. can baked beans
1 c. brown sugar

½ c. catsup
Bacon strips

Pour beans into casserole; add brown sugar and catsup and stir well. Place bacon strips on top. Bake in 350° oven for 1 hour and 15 minutes or until bacon is browned.

Nothing is so strong as gentleness; nothing so gentle as real strength.

MOTHER'S TUNA FISH CASSEROLE

A family favorite, just the way I learned from my mother. I dare not change it, but chopped onion or peas could be optional.

Small pkg. medium size noodles
1 can tuna fish
1 can mushroom soup

½ c. milk
Potato chips

Boil noodles in salted water until done and drain. Put in casserole. Add tuna fish, mushroom soup and milk, and mix well. Cover with crushed potato chips and bread crumbs. Bake in 350° oven for 30 minutes.

JUDY'S POTATOES AU GRATIN

Large bag frozen hash browns
16 oz. sour cream
1 to 2 c. grated cheese
2 cans potato soup

½ tsp. garlic salt
2 tsp. salt
¼ c. chopped onion

Mix all ingredients together except the potatoes, then mix with thawed potatoes. Dot with butter. Bake in greased pan or casserole for 1½ hours.

EASY OVEN SCALLOPED POTATOES
(Delicious!)

Layer of sliced potatoes, then onions and green peppers, mushroom soup that has been mixed with milk. Make in layers. Bake in 325° oven for 1½ hours.

SCALLOPED POTATOES AND HAM

Great for family, company, or pot lucks. Another favorite of my family.

7 Tbsp. cornstarch
3 c. milk
¼ stick margarine or butter

Salt and pepper to taste
1¼ to 1½ c. Velveeta cheese

Peel and slice fairly thin 6 medium potatoes. Boil slowly in lightly salted water while making sauce. Put cornstarch in pan, slowly add milk so mixture will be smooth. Add salt and pepper to taste and margarine; add cheese cut in hunks. Cook on medium heat constantly until mixture is real thick. Drain potatoes. In a 2 quart casserole, place a layer of potatoes, then a layer of sauce, then a layer of baked ham and repeat again. Pour remaining sauce to cover top. Bake at 350° for 30 minutes or until the cheese bubbles well.

CHICKEN CASSEROLE

Easy and Tasty

6 to 8 chicken breasts or 1 whole chicken, cooked and boned. Use the broth and mix with 1 box cubed dressing (ENOUGH BROTH to make cubed dressing real moist) Spread into 9x12 baking dish.

Cook 1 box Uncle Bens rice according to directions, then add cut up chicken. Spread this over the dressing. Mix 1 can mushroom soup and ¼ cup milk. Pour over dressing and bake for 45 minutes in 325 degree oven.

ESCALLOPED PINEAPPLE

Delicious and you'll be proud to serve this beautiful casserole.

1 (No. 2) can pineapple tidbits,
  drained (reserve juice)
1 c. Cheddar cheese chunks
¾ c. sugar
3 Tbsp. flour

1 tsp. butter or margarine
2 slices toast
¼ c. butter or margarine, melted
Maraschino cherries (optional)

In buttered casserole, place the pineapple that has been drained. Add the cheese. In small pan, place sugar and flour. Gradually add drained pineapple juice. Cook until thickened. Add 1 teaspoon butter. Stir until melted. Pour over pineapple and cheese and mix together. Break toast in small pieces and mix with the melted butter. Stir together and place on top of dish. Arrange halved maraschino cherries on top to add beauty. Bake 350 for 30 minutes.

To keep your marriage brimming,
With love in the loving cup.
Whenever you're wrong, admit it!
Whenever you're right, shut up.

MASHED POTATOES

9 potatoes, cooked and mashed
1 (8 oz.) pkg. cream cheese,
  softened
1 c. sour cream

1 tsp. garlic salt
1 tsp. onion salt
3 Tbsp. butter
⅛ tsp. paprika

Mix all ingredients with mixer. Pour in casserole. Bake ½ hour at 325°.

Note: This may be prepared ahead, but if refrigerated, bake 12 minutes longer.

Some Thrifty housewives who would say
That waste could cause them sorrow,
Will save leftover dabs today
But throw them out tomorrow.

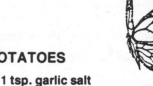

ZUCCHINI CASSEROLE

1 medium zucchini, chopped
1 medium onion, chopped
½ stick oleo
Salt and pepper to taste
⅛ c. water

⅔ can Cheddar cheese soup
1 can cream of chicken soup
¼ c. milk
1 c. cooked rice

Saute the zucchini and onion in oleo. Mix with other ingredients and put in casserole. Bake in 350° oven for 40 minutes.

41

BERTIE'S LIMA BEAN AND BROCCOLI CASSEROLE
(Extra special!)

Cook separately 1 (10 ounce) package baby lima beans and 1 (10 ounce) package broccoli.

Toss together and add to the above:

1 can mushroom soup
1 env. Lipton's onion soup mix
1 stick margarine, melted

1 c. sour cream
1 c. water chestnuts
3 c. Rice Krispies

Place lima beans and broccoli in casserole dish. Lightly toss mushroom soup, onion soup mix, sour cream and water chestnuts. Pour over first ingredients. Melt 1 stick margarine and add 3 cups Rice Krispies. Stir until well blended. Pour over top of soup mixture.

SWEET POTATO CASSEROLE

A delightful way to use sweet potatoes, this recipe was shared with me by my sister, Shirley Jean Acton. Especially good served with holiday meals.

3 c. mashed sweet potatoes
1 c. sugar
½ tsp. salt

2 eggs, beaten
½ c. milk
1 tsp. vanilla

Mix together and place in baking dish.

In a separate bowl, mix:

1 c. brown sugar
½ c. flour

1 c. chopped pecans
½ stick butter, melted

Mix until crumbly; add this to top of sweet potatoes. Bake at 400° for 35 minutes.

CORN SCALLOP

2 (No. 2) cans cream style yellow
    corn
2 c. milk
2 well beaten eggs

1½ c. cracker crumbs
½ c. minced onion
¼ c. butter or margarine, melted
1 c. cracker crumbs

Heat corn and milk. Gradually stir into eggs. Add 1½ cracker crumbs and onion. Pour into greased 2 quart casserole. Pour melted butter over 1 cup crumbs. Sprinkle over corn. Bake in 350° oven for 55 minutes.

SCALLOPED TOMATOES

3 c. tomatoes
¼ c. butter
3 c. bread crumbs
1 t. salt

⅛ t. pepper
⅛ t. allspice
    (Optional)
⅓ c. sugar

Heat tomatoes and butter. Mix in crumbs, sugar, salt, pepper, and allspice. Bake in buttered 9 x 9 baking dish in a 350 degree oven for 40 minutes.

TACO CASSEROLE

1 lb. ground beef
½ pkg. taco seasoning
1 can tomatoes
1 can red beans

Crushed corn chips
Pkg. Mozzarella cheese
Shredded lettuce
Chopped tomatoes

Brown ground beef and drain. Add taco seasoning. Drain tomatoes and bean juice and add to meat. Heat and pour into greased casserole. Crush corn chips and sprinkle over top. Add a package Mozzarella cheese. Bake at 350° for 15 minutes.

Remove from oven and spread shredded lettuce and diced raw tomatoes over top.

CORN OYSTER CASSEROLE

1 can cream corn
1 can whole kernel corn, drained
1 can oyster pieces

2 c. Ritz crackers, crumbled
½ c. milk

Stir all ingredients together. Bake at 325° for 30 minutes.

CHICKEN CASSEROLE SUPREME
(A delicious one-dish buffet meal)

4 to 6 lb. hen
4 cans cream of chicken soup
1 lb. spaghetti
1 can mushrooms
3 ribs celery, chopped fine

½ c. chopped onion
¼ c. bell pepper
2 Tbsp. chopped pimento
1 c. sharp grated cheese

Stew hen and save broth for spaghetti. Mix and pour into casserole. Saute oil or butter; add soup and chicken cut in bite-size pieces. Add mushrooms, celery, onion, pepper and pimento. Cook spaghetti in broth. Add to mixture. Mix and pour into casseroles. Can be made into 4 casseroles. Bake in 350° oven for 20 minutes. These may be frozen and used later. Heat in oven, top with sharp grated cheese.

COPPER PENNIES

Serve as a relish or as a vegetable.
An excellent dish, shared with me from my good friend and Neighbor Julie Charles, Marietta, Georgia.

2 lb. carrots, peeled and sliced
1 green pepper, chopped or strips
2 medium onions, sliced thin
1 can tomato soup
¾ cup sugar

½ oil
¾ c. vinegar
1 t. mustard
salt & pepper to taste
1 t. worcestershire sauce

Cook carrots till done but still crisp. Drain and place in layer in the bottom of a shallow bowl; add a layer of green peppers then onion rings. Repeat layers until all the vegetables are used. Combine remainder of called for ingredients. Mix well. Pour over vegetables. Let stand a few hours or overnight in refrigerator. Serve cold.

Note: Attractive served in a clear bowl. May heat in microwave for a delicious hot dish.

FOOTBALL STEW

Enjoy the game while dinner is cooking!

2 lb. stew meat, cut up	1 Tbsp. salt
6 carrots, cut fine	2 Tbsp. sugar
3 small onions	3 Tbsp. minute tapioca
1 c. celery, cut fine	1 can mushrooms (optional)
31 oz. can tomatoe juice	Noodles (optional)
3 potatoes, cut fine	2 Tbsp. Worcestershire Sauce

Do not brown meat. Mix all together and bake for 5 hours at 300 . Cook, covered. Can be served over cooked noodles.

WILD RICE

1 large onion, chopped	2 env. Lipton's chicken noodle soup
1 bunch celery, chopped	4½ c. water
1 green pepper, chopped	1 c. uncooked wild rice
1 lb. ground sausage	1 can mushroom soup

Saute sausage for 30 minutes. Pour off drippings, using enough to saute chopped vegetable. Then cook vegetables, rice, chicken soup in water 15 to 20 minutes, slowly. Add mushroom soup and meat and bake at 350° for 2 hours. Use covered casserole, placed in pan of water.

ASPARAGUS CASSEROLE

1 can asparagus spears	Bread crumbs
1 c. white sauce, seasoned	1 c. sharp cheese, grated
½ c. slivered almonds	

Melt ½ cup cheese in sauce. Grease 1½ quart casserole. Layer with white sauce, asparagus, almonds, rest of white sauce. Cover top with bread crumbs and rest of cheese. Bake 30 minutes uncovered at 350°

Remember thy Creator in the day of thy youth.
For the things that he teaches are full of mercy and truth.

SHIRLEY JEAN'S SPECIAL CARROT PUDDING
(Delicious!!)

2 c. mashed carrots
1 tsp. baking powder
2 Tbsp. flour
¼ tsp. cinnamon

3 eggs (whole), beaten
1 c. milk
1½ c. sugar

Melt ½ stick margarine in casserole. Cook carrots soft and mash and cool. Mix dry ingredients. Add eggs and milk and carrots and mix well. Add carrot mixture in butter in casserole. Bake in 325° oven for 45 minutes to 1 hour, till crusty on top. Best served with turkey, ham and etc.

MARINATED CARROTS

5 c. sliced carrots (2 lb.)
1 medium onion
1 small green pepper
1 c. sugar
½ c. vinegar
1 tsp. prepared mustard

1 tsp. salt
1 tsp. pepper
1 can tomato soup
½ c. salad oil
1 tsp. Worcestershire sauce

Cook carrots approximately 25 minutes, not overcooking. Cut onion in rings and green pepper in small pieces. Mix with other ingredients and pour over vegetables. Cover and marinate 12 hours. Drain and serve. Will keep for 2 weeks refrigerated.

TAMALE BAKE
(Excellent for potlucks, or guests)

¼ c. diced onion
¼ c. diced green pepper
½ c. diced celery
½ lb. ground beef
1 Tbsp. fat
¼ c. corn meal
1⅓ c. canned tomatoes

1 c. whole kernel corn
½ c. ripe olives
1½ tsp. chili powder
1½ tsp. salt
1½ tsp. Worcestershire sauce
½ c. grated cheese

Brown onion, green pepper, celery and ground beef in fat. Cook corn meal in tomatoes, 5 to 10 minutes; add meat mixture. Stir in corn, olives, and seasonings. Pour into 1½ quart casserole and top with grated cheese. Bake at 325° for 30 minutes.

SAUCY SPRING BAKE
(Wonderful for a brunch!)

1 (10 oz.) pkg. frozen asparagus,
     cooked and drained
1 (6 oz.) pkg. sliced Canadian bacon

2 (10½ oz.) cans chicken ala king
1 c. French fried onions

In shallow baking dish, arrange asparagus. Top with bacon. Pour ala king over it. Bake at 400° for 15 minutes. Top with onions and bake 5 minutes longer.

CHICKEN CASSEROLE

I have talked to women who say, ''I just do not do that much cooking anymore, I just do not have time.'' Hopefully, the recipes throughout this cookbook will be the answer for ''Today's Living.'' This can be put together in a few minutes and forgotten about until time to serve it. Place baked potatoes wrapped in aluminum foil in the oven with the casserole. Serve with a salad or applesauce and your meal is ready.

8 boned chicken breasts
8 dried beef slices (canned)

1 can mushroom soup
½ pt. sour cream

Roll beef and chicken and put in greased pan. Heat soup and sour cream together. Pepper to taste. Pour over chicken to cover. Bake at 200° for 3 hours.

The really happy man is the one who can enjoy the scenery when he has to take a detour.

NO-WORK CHICKEN
(So good and best prepared the day before.)

4 large chicken breasts
½ c. honey
½ c. Dijon style mustard

1 Tbsp. curry powder
2 Tbsp. soy sauce

Place chicken, skin side down, in a flat baking dish in one layer. In a small bowl, mix together remaining ingredients. Coat chicken; cover with foil and refrigerate overnight or for at least 6 hours. When ready to cook, turn chicken so skin side is up, recover with foil and bake at 350° for 1 hour or until done. Baste with sauce and cook uncovered during the last 15 minutes. When serving, spoon sauce over chicken. Makes 4 servings.

MUSHROOMS AND RICE
(Quick, and always good)

2⅔ c. packaged precooked rice
    (uncooked)
6 Tbsp. cooking oil
2 (4 oz.) cans button mushrooms,
    drained

1 bunch green onions, chopped
2 (10½ oz.) cans beef consomme
    (undiluted)
2 Tbsp. soy sauce
½ tsp. salt

Mix all ingredients together and bake, covered, at 350° until liquid is absorbed, approximately 30 to 35 minutes. Do not stir.

MARINATED CHUCK ROAST

3 to 4 lbs. boneless chuck roast
½ c. soy sauce

¼ c. honey
½ t. garlic powder

Combine soy sauce, honey and garlic powder. Pour over roast and refrigerate for 12 hours. Drain meat and bring to room temperature. Place on a rack in a shallow pan. Bake at 425 degrees to desired doneness. Cut in thin slices.

CRUNCHY CHICKEN CASSEROLE

Place 2½ to 3 pound chicken in kettle (or chicken parts you prefer). Cook until tender. Cut chicken into bite size chunks. Heat oven to 400 degrees. Combine chicken with the following:

2 cups chopped celery
1 small can black olives
2 Tbsp. grated onion
1 cup mayonnaise

½ cup chopped toasted peanuts
salt to taste
4 Tbsp. lemon juice

Pile lightly in casserole or individual dishes. Sprinkle with ½ cup grated cheese and 1 cup potato chip pieces. Bake 20 minutes for casserole, less for individual servings.

EGGPLANT, ZUCCHINI OR SQUASH CASSEROLE

2 c. cooked eggplant
1 Tbsp. chopped onion
6 Tbsp. butter
1 tsp. salt
1 c. cracker crumbs

1 c. cubed cheese
2 eggs, beaten
1 c. milk
¼ tsp. pepper
¼ tsp. sage

While eggplant is hot, drain and add ingredients. Put in casserole. Bake in 350° oven until center of mixture rises.

SEAFOOD CASSEROLE

1 (4½ oz.) can shrimp
1 (6½ oz.) can tuna fish
1 (7½ oz.) can crabmeat
2 (3 oz.) cans chow mein noodles
2 (10½ oz.) cans cream of
  mushroom soup

1⅓ c. water
2 c. celery, chopped
1 c. cashew nuts

Devein shrimp, if needed. Pour hot water over all seafood and drain. (Empty the contents of the cans into a sieve and pour hot water over all.) This cleans off any oil from the fish. Combine all ingredients. Spoon into a large casserole. A few of the chow mein noodles may be sprinkled on top. Bake at 350° for 30 minutes.

HAZEL'S FAVORITE ZUCCHINI
(With sour cream)

Delicious - good for family or company.

Peel zucchini. Cut into ½ inch slices and cook in salt water for five minutes. Drain well. Place in an 8 inch casserole dish. Mix together 1 cup sour cream, 1 cup grated Cheddar cheese, 1 tablespoon butter and heat until well blended. Pour over zucchini.

Topping: Mix ½ teaspoon salt, ½ cup bread crumbs, and 2 tablespoons grated cheese. Place on top. Bake in 375° oven for 10 minutes.

Happiness in the Heart puts Sunshine in the day.

SALMON LOAF
(Good and easy to make!)

1 large can salmon
7 crackers, rolled to crumbs

3 eggs
4 Tbsp. melted butter

Stir until smooth. Bake ½ hour at 400° in 8 or 9 inch baking dish.

Note: White sauce, mixed with catsup is great for a topping.

SPANISH DELIGHT

How many times have we found ourselves in search for an oven meal on a busy day? Add a salad to this casserole and you will have a fine meal.

1½ lb. hamburger
1 medium onion, chopped
1 green pepper, chopped
1 can tomato paste or sauce
1 small can mushrooms
1 (No. 2) can whole grain corn

1 tsp. salt
1 tsp. pepper
1 tsp. chili powder (optional)
Noodles
Cheese
Bread crumbs

Brown meat, onions and green pepper. Add tomato paste, mushrooms and corn. Cook for 15 to 20 minutes. Add salt, pepper and chili powder. Cook noodles in salted water and add to above mixture. Put in greased casserole. Top with cheese and bread crumbs. Bake for 45 minutes at 350°.

Have you heard the Mexican Weather Forecast? Chilli today, hot tamale.

VEGETABLE CASSEROLE

2 large pkg. mixed vegetables
 (broccoli, cauliflower and
 carrots)

1 lb. Velveeta cheese, cubed
1 tube Ritz crackers, crushed
1 stick butter

Cook vegetables. Melt butter and stir in crackers. Grease a 3 quart casserole, put vegetables in, add the cubed cheese on top and the cracker mixture on top of this. Bake in 350° oven for 20 minutes, or until cheese melts.

Love's a present
you can give,
every single day you live!

I Will sing of the Mercies of the Lord forever. Psalms 89:1

CHICKEN DELIGHT

A recipe from our daughter-in-law Jo Ellen, who finds cooking a real joy. She is a creative cook and likes to try new recipes. You'll enjoy this variation!

2 c. cooked chicken
½ c. bell pepper
½ c. chopped onion
2 Tbsp. shortening
1 Tbsp. minced garlic
½ c. chopped celery

½ c. mushrooms
1 small can tomatoes
1 small can tomato sauce
2 tsp. Italian seasoning
2 c. cooked rice, drained
1 c. Mozzarella cheese

Cook chicken and debone. Dice chicken and brown with the celery, pepper and onion in the 2 tablespoons shortening in electric skillet. Add minced garlic, mushrooms, tomatoes, tomato sauce and Italian seasoning. Mix all together and cook for 30 minutes on medium heat. Top with Mozzarella cheese. Place lid back on skillet till cheese melts. Put rice on platter and spoon chicken mixture over rice and serve immediately.

CHICKEN BROCCOLI CASSEROLE

Another delicious recipe you'll want to use often!

2 cans chicken soup
2 c. chicken breasts, diced
¾ c. grated cheese
2 pkg. frozen broccoli spears

Salt and pepper to taste
1 c. cracker crumbs
1 c. mayonnaise

Cook broccoli until half done; drain. Place in bottom of casserole dish. Add chicken. Mix soup and mayonnaise. Pour over the chicken. Grate cheese and sprinkle over top. Place cracker crumbs on top, with pats of butter across top. Bake, covered, in 350° oven for 45 minutes.

BROCCOLI CASSEROLE

1 chopped onion, sauteed
½ stick margarine
1 pkg. California mix, cooked and drained
1 c. Minute rice

1 can mushroom soup, or soup of your choice
¼ c. water
½ c. milk
½ c. cheese

Saute onion in margarine. Mix all ingredients together and place in casserole. Bake in 350° oven for 35 minutes.

A WONDERFUL STREUSEL TOPPING FOR MOST ANY CASSEROLE

½ c. Bisquick baking mix
¼ c. chopped nuts
¼ c. grated Parmesan cheese

⅛ tsp. garlic powder
2 Tbsp. butter

Mix ingredients together, cutting in butter. Place crumbled topping on casseroles.

VEGETABLE CASSEROLE

1 can wax beans
1 can green beans
2 c. celery strips
2½ c. carrot strips
2 c. stewed tomatoes
3 Tbsp. tapioca

1 small onion, chopped
½ green pepper, chopped
1½ Tbsp. sugar
1½ tsp. salt
Pepper to taste

Mix all together, cover and bake in 350° oven for 2 hours.

GREEN BEAN CASSEROLE

A casserole easily fixed to slip in the oven ½ hour before serving dinner.

2 cans green beans, drained
1 (6 oz.) can sliced mushrooms,
    drained
1 can mushroom soup
1 diced green pepper

1 small jar pimento
½ tsp. salt
Pepper to taste
½ c. chopped almonds
French fried onion rings

Mix all ingredients together, except onion rings. Bake for 15 minutes in 350° oven and then add onion rings and bake 15 minutes longer or until bubbly.

Let others share your sunny days
and you will find it true,
that others will be glad to share
the rainy days with you.

POTATO CASSEROLE

A recipe from my friend, Judy Shaefer who lives in Phoenix, Ar. Judy is an enthusiastic golfer and also enjoys cooking.

2 lb. frozen hash browns
1 large ctn. sour cream
10 oz. shredded Cheddar cheese
½ c. chopped onion

1 tsp. salt
1 tsp. pepper
1 can cream of mushroom soup

Blend all together. Top with 3 cups crushed potato chips, onion rings or crushed corn flakes. Bake in 350° oven for 1 hour.

For fluffier mashed potatoes, add a pinch of baking soda, as well as milk and butter.

A well beaten white of an egg added to mashed potatoes will add to the looks and taste of the potatoes.

When cooking spaghetti or rice, put butter in the water to keep spaghetti and rice from sticking.

Mix ½ cup tomato sauce with ½ cup of water to make 1 cup of tomato juice.

BEEF JERKEY
(Perfect for the outdoorsman!)

1 (5 to 6 lb.) brisket
1 c. Worcestershire sauce
1 c. soy sauce
1 tsp. garlic powder

1 tsp. onion powder
1 tsp. salt
1 tsp. pepper

Trim all the fat you can from the meat. Semi-freeze the meat so it can be sliced easily. Slice into thin strips. For the marinade, combine all the ingredients except the meat. Marinate the meat in a 9x13 inch shallow glass dish in refrigerator overnight. Layer meat in the dish and cover meat with marinade sauce. Lay strips of marinated meat in a single layer on rack in oven. The strips may touch, but not overlap. A cookie sheet should be placed under the rack to catch the drips. Since the meat is so lean, the drip is not excessive. Set oven at lowest possible temperature. Leave oven door open slightly. During the latter part of cooking, (about 8 hours) taste occasionally to determine the degree of chewiness desired. Some like beef jerky crisp, some like it chewier.

Beef jerky is served at room temperature. To store, place jerky in glass jars with the lids on tight, or in a moisture-proof plastic airtight plastic bag. Jerky will keep for 6 months. It retains more flavor if stored at refrigerator temperature. This beef jerky is not for anyone on a salt restricted diet.

MOTHER'S CHOP SUEY

3 Tbsp. oil or bacon fat
2 lb. cubed lean beef
1 c. sliced onion
2 c. diced celery
1 (4 oz.) can mushrooms, drained
1 can bean sprouts, drained

2 Tbsp. cornstarch
2¼ c. water
1½ tsp. salt
1 Tbsp. bead molasses
2 Tbsp. soy sauce

Heat fat in skillet preheated to 350°. Add beef and brown lightly. Add onions, celery, mushrooms, cook about 3 minutes. Mix cornstarch until smooth with ¼ cup water and add remaining water, salt, molasses and soy sauce to meat mixture. Reduce heat to low and simmer, covered, until meat is tender. Add drained bean sprouts and continue cooking until heated through. Serve on hot fluffy rice.

Note: Mix any leftover chop suey with rice and serve later.

In quietness and confidence shall be your strength. Isaiah 30:15

BEEF CUBED STEAKS
(Tasty topping)

4 beef cubed steaks	¼ c. catsup
2 Tbsp. cooking fat	2 Tbsp. chopped green onion
½ tsp. salt	¼ c. shredded Cheddar cheese

Brown steaks on both sides in fat for 7 to 10 minutes. Pour off drippings. Top each steak with ⅛ teaspoon salt, 1 tablespoon catsup, 1½ teaspoon onion and 1 tablespoon shredded cheese. Cover and cook over low heat 2 to 3 minutes. Makes 4 servings.

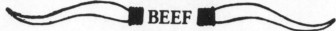

MAMA'S MEATLOAF

For a variation of meat loaf try this.

¾ c. corn flakes or crushed crackers	¼ tsp. celery seed
½ c. milk	1 Tbsp. dried parsley
1 (10½ oz.) can mushroom soup	1 tsp. Worcestershire sauce
1 soup can milk	½ onion, finely chopped
1 lb. ground beef	1 egg, well beaten
1 tsp. salt	1½ Tbsp. catsup
⅛ tsp. pepper	1½ Tbsp. barbecue sauce

Soak corn flakes in ½ cup milk until soft. Heat mushroom soup and soup can of milk for sauce. Mix corn flakes and all other ingredients together in a 2 quart casserole dish and shape into loaf. Pour ½ of the sauce over loaf. Bake at 350°. After 15 minutes of cooking, pour remaining sauce over loaf and continue baking for 25 minutes. Serves 6.

SPARERIBS AND SAUERKRAUT
(A flavor combination that is special!)

3 to 4 lb. country style spareribs, or pork roast	2 Tbsp. brown sugar
1 large can sauerkraut	1 apple sliced and cored (optional)
	1 tsp. caraway seed (optional)

Cook spareribs in boiling water until tender. Allow to set overnight, in the refrigerator. Remove the fat over top the spareribs before heating the next morning. Add large can sauerkraut with brown sugar and sliced apples. Simmer for 45 minutes.

"Usually spareribs are very greasy. Cooking them the day before one uses them, eliminates this problem."

Convenience foods are handy
And I use them now with ease
But for special times I still rely
On favorite receipes.

GOURMET PORK CHOPS
(Scrumptious!)

6 pork chops
2 Tbsp. flour
1 tsp. salt and dash of pepper
2 Tbsp. shortening
1 (10½ oz.) can condensed cream
   of mushroom soup

½ tsp. ground ginger
¼ tsp. dried rosemary, crushed
1 (3½ oz.) can French fried onions
½ c. sour cream

Coat chops with a mixture of salt, flour and pepper. In skillet brown on both sides in hot shortening. Place in 11 x 7 x 1½ inch baking dish. Combine soup, ¾ cup water, ginger, and rosemary. Pour over chops. Sprinkle with half the onions. Cover and bake at 350° for 50 minutes, or until meat is tender. Uncover; sprinkle with remaining onions and continue baking 10 minutes. Remove meat to platter. Blend sour cream into soup mixture; heat. Serve with meat.

Did is a work of achievement.
Won't is a word of retreat.
Can't is a word of duty.
Can is a word of power.

LASAGNA

"This casserole may be made ahead of time and refrigerated until baking time. Makes 10 or more servings."

1½ lb. hamburger
1½ tsp. salt
⅛ tsp. pepper
1 onion, diced
¼ tsp. garlic salt or fresh garlic
1 (32 oz) bottle Ragu spaghetti
   sauce with mushrooms

1 (15 oz.) can tomato sauce
1 (6 oz) can tomato paste
1 lb. small curd cottage cheese
2 eggs
¾ c. Parmesan cheese
1 lb. pkg. Mozzarella cheese
Lasagna noodles

Brown meat with onion, spices, and sauces. Simmer for 2 hours, stirring occasionally. While sauce is simmering boil noodles; drain and rinse in cold water. Mix 2 eggs beaten with cottage cheese, Parmesan cheese. In oblong casserole, layer meat sauce, noodles, cottage cheese mixture, meat, Mozzerella cheese, noodles, meat. Bake until good and hot.

STEAMED BEEF BRISKET

6 - 10 lbs. beef brisket
2 Tbsp. Liquid smoke

3 Tbsp. water
1 package dried onion soup mix

Wipe brisket dry and lay in a roasting pan. Pour Liquid Smoke and water in bottom of pan. Spread onion soup mix over top of brisket. Tightly cover with foil. Bake at 250 degrees for 5 hours. Cut in thin slices.

Note: An electric knife is best for cutting brisket, rump and sirloin tip roasts.

ROUND REUBEN PIZZA

It was a joy, as Tillie Astorino of West Adams, Ma. shared this recipe with me, in which she won the $32,000.00 Grand Prize in a Cheesefeast Lifestyle recipe contest. If you like Reuben sandwiches and rice, you'll win raves when you serve it too!

5 c. cooked rice
1 c. shredded Swiss cheese
¼ c. grated Parmesan cheese
2 eggs, beaten
2 tsp. caraway seed
2 (8 oz.) pkg. cream cheese,
  softened
2 Tbsp. horseradish mustard
1 (16 oz.) can sauerkraut, drained
  and rinsed

½ lb. sliced corned beef, cut into
  strips
2 c. shredded Swiss cheese
¼ c. grated Parmesan cheese
⅓ c. pitted ripe olive slices
¼ c. chopped pimento, drained
¼ c. chopped parsley

Combine rice, Swiss and Parmesan cheese, eggs and caraway seed; mix well. Press onto bottom and sides of 12 inch greased pizza pan. Bake at 450° for 15 to 18 minutes or until lightly browned. Combine cream cheese and mustard, mixing until well blended. Spread over crust. Layer sauerkraut, meat, Swiss and Parmesan cheese over cream cheese mixture. Bake at 450° for 10 minutes or until cheese is melted. Top with olives, pimento and parsley. Serves 8.

SAVORY OVEN POT ROAST

After discovering the good flavoring of Lawry's seasoning salt, I hardly ever bake a roast without it, a delicious blending of flavors.

3 to 4 lb. rump or round tip roast
2 tsp. Lawry's seasoned salt
Pepper to taste
1 tsp. garlic powder
1 tsp. onion powder

½ stick margarine
1 c. water
Potatoes, peeled
Carrots, scrubbed, but not peeled

Make slits in roast and cover with Lawry's seasoned salt, pepper, garlic powder and onion powder. Put margarine and water in pan with roast. Bake, covered, at 325° for 4 hours, basting the roast 2 times. After 3 hours, add potatoes and carrots.

Note: When done, thicken juice for gravy.

Stuff it and roast it, baste it with care,
Carefully then some gravy prepare,
Around your kitchen savory odors will tell,
Whatever is cooking, is doing quite well.

STEAK CHOW MEIN

2 lb. round steak, cubed
2 large onions, diced
2 tsp. soy sauce
Salt and pepper to taste
1 tsp. chili powder

5 stalks celery, chopped
½ green pepper, diced
2 cans bean sprouts
Chow mein noodles

Brown steak and onions in soy sauce and season with salt and pepper to taste. Cover and simmer until steak is tender, about 2 hours. Remove to a deep saucepan. Add chili powder and celery. Cook 30 minutes. Add green peppers and bean sprouts. Simmer at least 2 hours. Serve over chow mein noodles. May need to add liquid while simmering.

SPAGHETTI AND MEATBALLS

Upon requests for my spaghetti and meatballs recipe, I've decided to put to a recipe the procedure and ingredients I use. Served with a salad and French bread, makes a meal in itself and you will see that it does not take to long to prepare. When I ask our sons what I should fix for dinner, many times the answer is spaghetti and meatballs. Hope you like them too!

1½ lb. ground chuck
1 c. bread crumbs or cracker
    crumbs
3 eggs
1½ tsp. salt
¼ tsp. pepper
½ c. catsup

7 sections of garlic bud
2 medium onions
Cooking oil
16 oz. can tomato sauce
8 oz. can tomato paste
1 qt. tomato juice
3 Tbsp. sugar

Mix the first 6 ingredients together with one onion, chopped fine and make into small meatballs. Brown meatballs on both sides in skillet in ¼ inch of cooking oil. While these are browning, in small pan cook the other onion chopped fine, and the 7 sections of the garlic bud chopped fine, in enough oil to cover the bottom of the small pan. After cooked until tender, drain and add to the sauce, paste, juice and sugar. Mix well in large pan, stirring occasionally and bring to boil. Reduce temperature and add meatballs to sauce, cooking slowly for around 30 minutes. As this cooks, cook spaghetti until done and let simmer until ready to drain and serve with the meatballs and sauce.

Note: ¼ teaspoon Italian Seasoning in the sauce is good. For a quick sauce without meatballs, simply brown ground chuck and onion with salt and pepper. Add Prego sauce and serve with spaghetti.

FLOYD'S RUMP ROAST

Trim all fat from a 6-8 lb. roast
Cut 4 holes in each side of roast.
Insert small piece of garlic in each hole.
Rub entire roast with brown sugar.
Brown entire roast in Dutch oven or deep open skillet in oil.
Add ½ pkg. onion soup mix or 1 sliced onion.
Cover and cook slowly 2 to 3 hours or until tender.
Cool roast before slicing.

MICROWAVE MEAT LOAF

2 lb. hamburger
2 slices bread
¼ tsp. pepper
1 (8 oz.) can tomato sauce
1 chopped onion

1½ tsp. salt
2 eggs
1½ Tbsp. brown sugar
1 Tbsp. prepared mustard

Break up bread in small pieces. Mix all ingredients. Put in greased microwave ring mold. Cook 10 minutes on HIGH, turn directions and cook ten minutes more.

SWEDISH MEAT BALLS

2 lb. hamburger
⅔ c. oatmeal (uncooked)
1 small onion, diced

1 c. milk
¼ tsp. salt

Mix together and form into 2 inch balls. Place in 9x13 inch pan.

Make a sauce of:

¼ c. brown sugar
3 Tbsp. vinegar
1 c. catsup

1 c. water
1 small onion, diced

Blend and pour over meatballs. Bake at 350° for 1 hour.

FOOL THE WORLD CATFISH

This can be a fun recipe to make. Try it and hear the replies you receive. Tastes exactly like catfish.

2 c. flake hominy, cooked
1 tsp. salt
1 egg

1 tall can salmon, rinsed
Corn meal

After cooking the hominy, cool and add salt. Add egg, salmon; make into long cakes and roll in corn meal. Fry very crisp.

COMPANY MEATBALLS

2 lbs. ground beef
1 c. sour cream
1 pkg. dry onion soup mix
1 egg, slightly beaten
1 ½ c. dry coarse bread crumbs
⅓ c. flour

1 t. paprika
¼ c. butter
1 can cream of chicken soup
¼ c. water

Mix beef, sour cream, soup mix, egg and crumbs. Form into ball size of walnut. Mix flour and paprika; roll balls in mixture. Brown slowly on all sides in butter. Blend soup and water; pour over meat. Cover pan and simmer for about 20 minutes.

"Prayer is the Key that unlocks many doors."

SUNDAY CHICKEN

Chicken pieces of your choice (or 2
   young chickens, cut up)

   Sauce:

1 large onion
1 small can mushrooms
1 small green pepper
1 tsp. garlic powder

Salt, pepper, flour
4 Tbsp. salad oil

1 small can tomato juice and 1 can
   water
1 tsp. salt
1 tsp. sugar

Sprinkle cut up chicken with flour, salt, and pepper. Brown lightly in salad oil.

Sauce: Cook vegetables in shortening until almost brown. Add tomato juice, water, and seasoning. Pour sauce over chicken, cover and cook slowly until chicken is tender; about 35 to 40 minutes.

Cook on Saturday, heat on Sunday while the vegetables are cooking.

RICE AND CHICKEN CASSEROLE

1 can chicken soup
1 can celery soup
1 can mushroom soup
¾ c. water
1 (6 oz.) pkg. Uncle Ben's long grain and
   wild rice

Chicken thighs and breasts, or one
   whole chicken, skinned

Mix soups, water and rice. Pour into 9x13 inch baking dish. Put chicken pieces on top. Dot with butter. Bake in 275° oven covered for 2½ hours and uncovered for ½ hour if desire to have lightly browned.

good!

BAKED CHICKEN
(Easy! Delicious!)

8 to 10 chicken breasts, thighs, or
   drumsticks
1 pkg. dried onion soup mix

1 c. water
8 oz. French dressing
8 oz. apricot jam

Mix last 4 ingredients together in a blender. Skin chicken and put in flat pan. Pour ½ mixture over chicken. Bake ¾ hour at 325°. Turn pieces and pour rest over and bake another ½ hour or until tender.

CHUCK ROAST

2 or 3 lb. roast
Salt

1 can cream of mushroom soup
½ c. dry Lipton's onion soup

Pour a can of mushroom soup into bottom of roaster. Salt the roast and place over soup. Sprinkle the onion soup over this. Cover roast and cook 3 to 4 hours at 300°.

MEAT MARINADE FOR STEAK, KABOBS OR CHICKEN
(Delicious! Grill, broil or bake)

½ c. soy sauce
½ c. oil
4 Tbsp. catsup

2 Tbsp. vinegar
½ tsp. pepper
4 cloves garlic, crushed

Mix thoroughly. Marinate 2 to 24 hours. Cook until tender, but not dry.

BEEF ENCHILADAS

2 lb. lean ground beef
1 Tbsp. oil
1 Tbsp. chili powder
1 tsp. salt

1 (15 oz.) can tomato sauce
1 large onion
1 lb. cheese
2 doz. tortillas

Chop onion and grate cheese and set aside. Heat skillet with cooking oil; add beef, chili powder, salt and pepper. Cook until done, but not brown. Add tomato sauce and heat. Moisten one tortilla at a time in meat-tomato mixture. Then place tortilla in a square or oblong pan. Place one heaping tablespoon of meat mixture along center of tortilla and top with cheese and onion. Roll the tortilla and turn edge of tortilla toward pan. Fill pan with rolled tortillas then sprinkle remaining meat mixture, onion and cheese over the tortillas. Meat mixture should be kept warm during the above steps. Heat in 350° oven for 15 minutes or until cheese is melted.

Note: Use a can of chili and put ½ can of water with it and add to the top of the tortillas after you put them in the pan. It helps keep them moist.

HAWAIIAN HAM

Very good over rice or buttered noodles.

½ c. brown sugar
2 Tbsp. cornstarch
½ tsp. salt
⅓ c. vinegar
1 c. pineapple juice
1 Tbsp. soy sauce

2 lb. smoked ham, cut in cubes
½ c. thinly sliced onion
1 c. thick green pepper strips
1 (No. 2) can pineapple chunks or
    tidbits

Combine first 6 ingredients in saucepan and cook until mixture is clear and slightly thick, stirring constantly. Place ham in bean pot or casserole. Add onion slices, green pepper strips and pineapple. Pour sauce over and bake. Bake in 2 quart baking dish in 350° oven for 1½ hours.

Ask, and it shall be given you;
Seek and you shall find;
Knock, and it shall be opened to you. (Matthew 7:7)

PEPPER STEAK

A recipe from our niece, Connie Alexander, from Potomac, Il. who is a school teacher, musician and homemaker. This recipe is a delightful meat dish, serve over rice.

1½ lb. round steak, cut in pieces
Paprika
Margarine
Garlic salt
1 can beef consomme

1 can onion soup
2 green peppers, cut in strips
¼ c. water with ¼ c. soy sauce
2 Tbsp. cornstarch

Sprinkle paprika over meat and allow to stand a few minutes. Brown both sides of meat in margarine. Add consomme and onion soup. Sprinkle on garlic salt. Cover and simmer 30 minutes. Stir in green peppers. Cover and cook 5 minutes. Blend cornstarch, water and soy sauce. Stir into meat mixture. Cook over low heat until thickened and clear, about 2 minutes.

MEAT-ZA-PIE

Enjoy making this today. A good flavor, easy to make, this recipe was shared to me from our sister-in-law Lorraine Remole, from Potomac, Il.

1 lb. ground beef
¼ tsp. garlic salt
¼ tsp. salt
Dash of pepper
1 egg
1 small onion, diced

⅓ c. catsup
2 or 3 slices American cheese
12 oz. can sliced mushrooms,
   drained
2 Tbsp. grated Parmesan cheese
½ tsp. oregano, crumbled fine

Combine meat, salts, pepper, egg and onion and pat over the bottom and sides of an 8 inch pie pan. Cut cheese in strips and place on top of catsup. Put on mushrooms, Parmesan cheese and oregano. Bake in 350° oven for 25 minutes. Cut in wedges to serve.

FAVORITE CHILI

Surprisingly good. Shared with me from a friend, Marie Bond from Excello, Missouri.

2 lb. hamburger
¾ c. chopped onion
2 (10½ oz.) cans cream of
   tomato soup
¼ tsp. minced garlic

2½ tsp. chili powder
1 tsp. salt
¼ tsp. pepper
2 (1 lb.) cans hot chili beans

Brown hamburger and onion and add garlic. Add seasonings, soup and hot beans. Stir to a boil, cover and simmer slowly for 30 minutes. Stir occasionally. Add water to desired consistency.

Friends are a treasured gift.

BARBECUED STEAK

A simple to make recipe that has been successful for years, I've enjoyed sharing this delicious meat dish.

2 lb. round steak (or more), cut in
   serving pieces
Salt

Pepper
Flour
½ c. oil

Trim all fat from steak. Salt and pepper each piece and flour on both sides. Brown on both sides in oil. Layer in casserole alternately with the barbecue sauce.

Barbecue sauce:
9 Tbsp. white sugar
3 Tbsp. brown sugar

4 tsp. celery seed
7 Tbsp. Worcestershire sauce
4½ c. catsup

Bake in oven at 350° for 1 hour.

COUNTRY STEAK AND CREAM OF ONION GRAVY

"What a quickie meat and gravy dish! Serve with mashed potatoes or baked. You may substitute venison steak for the beef."

2 lb. round steak, cut in serving
   pieces
1 tsp. salt
¼ tsp. pepper
½ c. vegetable oil

2 cans Campbell's cream of onion
   soup
1 c. water
Flour

Trim all fat from steak; roll in flour and brown in oil in skillet. Add seasoning. When browned, put in slow cooker, then add cream of onion soup and water. Let cook slowly for 3 to 4 hours.

Note: (Can make as an oven dish, using ½ can water instead of whole can, and baking at 300° for 1½ hours.)

HAM LOAF

Makes 20 individual loaves. Freeze some Excellent.

2 lbs. ground ham
1 lb. mild sausage
1 lb. hamburger
2 c. fine cracker crumbs
4 T. chopped onion
4 T. chopped celery

1 t. salt
½ t. pepper
2 cups milk
4 eggs

Mix well and form into individual loaves.

SWEET AND SOUR SAUCE TOPPING

1 c. brown sugar
½ c. catsup
½ c. vinegar

2 t. prepard mustard
½ c. water

Mix well and pour over individual loaves.

BARBECUED BRISKET
(Tender and juicy)

5 or 6 lb. brisket (request from butcher)
3 oz. liquid smoke
Garlic salt
Onion salt

Celery salt
Salt and pepper
Worcestershire sauce
6 oz. barbecue sauce

Place brisket on baking sheet or covered pan. Pour liquid smoke over meat and sprinkle generously with celery salt, onion salt and garlic salt. Cover pan with foil, place in refrigerator and marinate overnight or at least 6 hours. Before baking, pour off liquid and sprinkle with salt, pepper, and Worcestershire sauce. Replace foil. Bake 5 to 7 hours in a 275° oven. Remove from oven; pour barbecue sauce over meat, and bake one more hour. Allow to cool before slicing in thin slices.

Why does everyone want to be in the front of the bus, the rear of the church, and the middle of the road?

LIVER STROGANOFF
(A little extra oomph!)

1 lb. liver
Flour
Salt and pepper
½ stick butter or margarine (¼ c.)

½ c. sliced onion
½ c. sliced mushrooms
1 c. sour cream (room temperature)

Cut liver into ½ inch strips; dip in flour, season with salt and pepper. Melt butter in large, heavy skillet. Lightly saute onions and mushrooms; add liver. Brown on all sides quickly. Cover; cook over low heat about 10 minutes. Blend in sour cream; serve immediately. Serve stroganoff over rice or noodles, accompanied by broccoli or asparagus, and a salad.

"He who is faithful in a very little thing is faithful also in much." Luke 16:10

CHEESY CHICKEN WINGS
(Delicious to serve at parties or any occasion)

2 lb. chicken wings, disjointed
1 c. Parmesan cheese, grated
2 Tbsp. parsley
2 tsp. paprika

1 Tbsp. oregano
2 tsp. salt
½ tsp. pepper
½ c. melted butter

Discard tips of chicken wings, using only the large pieces. Mix together cheese and spices. Dip pieces in butter, then roll in cheese mixture. Place on a foil lined cookie sheet, forming a lip with foil. Bake for 1 hour and 15 minutes in 350° oven.

I Will sing of the Mercies of the Lord forever. Psalms 89:1

"Please Lord, fill my mouth with worthwhile stuff, and nudge me when I've said enough."

MISSOURI FRIED CHICKEN

Upon requests for my crispy fried chicken recipe, this is easy and another favorite of my family.

Chicken parts as preferred　　　　**Pepper (optional)**
Salt　　　　　　　　　　　　　　　**Oil or Crisco**
Flour

Wash and drain chicken. Cut off excess fat. Salt each piece of chicken and flour well. Let set 10 minutes, then flour again and place into the pan. The cooking oil should be a good ½ inch deep, at least. It shouldn't be smoking hot but hot enough. Brown pieces on all sides well, then turn the heat down slightly and keep on cooking until the chicken tests tender. Do not cover the pan with lid or you will lose all the crispness. Everything depends on having the shortening deep enough, and the right temperature.

"The wonderful world of home appliances now makes it possible to cook indoors with charcoal and outdoors with gas."

ITALIAN BEEF

A delicious blending of flavors! This recipe is from our niece Chris Hird who lives at Catlin, II. She is also a homemaker and enjoys cooking.

5 lb. chuck roast　　　　　　　　**1 onion, chopped**
½ c. vinegar　　　　　　　　　　 **1 green pepper, chopped**
½ c. water (if needed)　　　　　 **2 Tbsp. Tabasco sauce**
2 tsp. oregano　　　　　　　　　 **2 Tbsp. Worcestershire sauce**
Garlic clove　　　　　　　　　　 **1 pkg. brown gravy mix**

Cook roast until done. Add all other ingredients to broth. Cut or shred meat and put back into sauce. Cook slowly 4 to 8 hours.

GOLFER'S BEEF STEW

Go ahead and go golfing. Dinner will be ready in a few hours!

2 lb. beef chuck roast, or equal　　　**1 Tbsp. salt**
**　　amount of lean stew meat**　　　　**3 Tbsp. tapioca**
5 medium potatoes (small cubes)　　**1 slice bread, crumbled**
2 medium onions, chopped　　　　　**2 Tbsp. brown sugar**
1 medium turnip (optional)　　　　　**¼ c. water**
2 stalks celery, chopped　　　　　　**31 oz. can tomatoes or tomato juice**

Cut beef into bite-size pieces. Combine all ingredients in 4 quart baking dish, then cover. Bake in preheated 250° oven for about 7 hours.

♡ Husband to wife, "Honey, will you bring me my golf socks?" Reply, "Your golf socks?" "Yes, the ones with the 18 holes."

Our 10 year old grandson, Brent, contributed this one. "Why did the golfer wear 2 pairs of pants?" (In case he got a hole in one.)

PIZZA BURGERS

Real good and a quick way to serve hungry children! Yes, big kids, too!

3 lb. hamburger (or less)
1 pkg. Mozzarella cheese, shredded
Ragu Quick spaghetti sauce

1 tsp. Italian seasoning (add more if stronger flavor desired)

Brown hamburger in fry pan. Moisten well with Ragu Quick spaghetti sauce. Add Italian flavor and mix well. Place hamburger bun halves or English muffin halves on foil lined cookie sheet or sheets, depending on how many you wish to make. Place sauce on top of each bun and cover with Mozzarella cheese. Place in 350° oven until cheese melts across top.

JOHN MAZETTI

Makes a complete meal with a salad and garlic bread. Can be frozen ahead before baked.

1 lb. ground beef
2 onions
1 green pepper
Salt
Pepper
1 tsp. marjoram

1 can tomato soup
1 can tomatoes
½ c. grated cheese
8 oz. dry noodles
1 sm. jar of sliced mushroom

Brown the hamburger, onions and green pepper together, not letting it get too brown. Add tomato soup and tomatoes, cooking a few minutes. Add mushrooms and marjoram and cook until it thickens. Add cheese, then drained noodles, mixing all together and placing in casserole. Bake, uncovered, 20 to 25 minutes in 350° oven.

MEATLOAF

Simple to put together. Delicious.

1 or 1½ lb. lean ground beef
½ pkg. Lipton onion soup
1 c. oatmeal or cracker crumbs

2 eggs
Salt and pepper to taste
½ c. catsup

Mix well and bake in greased baking dish for 1 hour in 350° oven.

The most skillful flattery is to let a person talk on, and be a listener.

GOULASH

As a new bride, my grandmother showed me how to make this quick meat dish. As our six sons were growing, I had my own personal taxi service, driving to and from school often, to ball practice, piano lessons, taking meals to the field, chasing for implement parts, among many more functions. After my runs for the day, I fixed this recipe many times that always pleased my family. Of course, I've made the recipe in larger amounts!!

1½ lb. hamburger
1 medium onion
1 (8 oz.) pkg. elbow macaroni
1 (14 oz.) bottle catsup (or more to
     taste)

⅓ c. water
3 Tbsp. sugar

Boil macaroni while browning hamburger and onion together. Drain macaroni, adding to hamburger mixture. Add catsup, sugar and water to mixture and mix well. Heat through thoroughly and serve.

TURKEY AND DRESSING

As we were growing up Dad and mother raised a lot of turkeys. In those days it was unusual to see a turkey farm. People would drive for miles to view all the turkeys. Mother dressed many turkeys. I remember a round tub of boiling water, all ready to dress the turkeys and guess who fell in it. Yes, I did! Ooh, how that did hurt! With soda on my hands and arms, I was taken to the Doctor several miles away. I sure had everyone's attention that day. The experiences and memories are many of the years we raised turkeys. Turkey is still one of my favorite meats of my family. I'd like to tell you the easy way that I fix turkey and dressing.

Turkey:

Wash turkey and rinse inside very well. Salt inside of the turkey with approximately 2 tablespoons salt. Salt outside well, under wings and etc. Place in large roaster with tight lid.

For a 17-23 pound turkey, bake in 250° oven for 7 hours. (I usually bake this one during night.) For a 12-16 pound turkey, bake in 300° oven for 4½ - 5 hours.

Note: I like to dribble hot broth over turkey before serving.

Dressing:

3 c. celery, chopped
1 large or 2 medium onions, chopped
½ c. oil
1 loaf bread

4 Tbsp. sage
Salt and pepper
2 c. turkey broth
2 c. hot water

In pan, saute celery and onions. Pour over broken bread pieces in large bowl. Put sage across this. Pour hot broth and water over bread, celery, onions and sage and mix well. If too dry add a little water. Mix well. Add salt to taste. Place in baking dish or pan and bake for 1 hour in 350° oven.

Note: The amount of sage is a personal taste. If you have a smoker, try smoking a turkey. A turkey turns out beautiful garnished with lettuce leaves, grapes and so forth.

64

Breads
and
Jellies

FOOD QUANTITIES FOR 25, 50, AND 100 SERVINGS

FOOD	25 SERVINGS	50 SERVINGS	100 SERVINGS
Rolls	4 doz.	8 doz.	16 doz.
Bread	50 slices or 3 1-lb. loaves	100 slices or 6 1-lb. loaves	200 slices or 12 1-lb. loaves
Butter	½ pound	¾ to 1 pound	1½ pounds
Mayonnaise	1 cup	2 to 3 cups	4 to 6 cups
Mixed Filling for Sandwiches (meat, eggs, fish)	1½ quarts	2½ to 3 quarts	5 to 6 quarts
Mixed Filling (sweet-fruit)	1 quart	1¾ to 2 quarts	2½ to 4 quarts
Jams & Preserves	1½ lb.	3 lb.	6 lb.
Crackers	1½ lb.	3 lb.	6 lb.
Cheese (2 oz. per serving)	3 lb.	6 lb.	12 lb.
Soup	1½ gal.	3 gal.	6 gal.
Salad Dressings	1 pt.	2½ pt.	½ gal.
Meat, Poultry or Fish:			
Wieners (beef)	6½ pounds	13 pounds	25 pounds
Hamburger	9 pounds	18 pounds	35 pounds
Turkey or chicken	13 pounds	25 to 35 pounds	50 to 75 pounds
Fish, large whole (round)	13 pounds	25 pounds	50 pounds
Fish, fillets or steaks	7½ pounds	15 pounds	30 pounds
Salads, Casseroles, Vegetables:			
Potato Salad	4¼ quarts	2¼ gallons	4½ gallons
Scalloped Potatoes	4½ quarts or 1 12x20" pan	8½ quarts	17 quarts
Mashed Potatoes	9 lb.	18-20 lb.	25-35 lb.
Spaghetti	1¼ gallons	2½ gallons	5 gallons
Baked Beans	¾ gallon	1¼ gallons	2½ gallons
Jello Salad	¾ gallon	1¼ gallons	2½ gallons
Canned Vegetables	1 #10 can	2½ #10 cans	4 #10 cans
Fresh Vegetables:			
Lettuce (for salads)	4 heads	8 heads	15 heads
Carrots (3 oz. or ½ c.)	6¼ lb.	12½ lb.	25 lb.
Tomatoes	3-5 lb.	7-10 lb.	14-20 lb.
Desserts:			
Watermelon	37½ pounds	75 pounds	150 pounds
Fruit Cup (½ c. per serving)	3 qt.	6 qt.	12 qt.
Cake	1 10x12" sheet cake 1½ 10" layer cakes	1 12x20" sheet cake 3 10" layer cakes	2 12x20" sheet cakes 6 10" layer cakes
Whipping Cream	¾ pint	1½ to 2 pints	3 pints
Ice Cream:			
Brick	3¼ quarts	6½ quarts	12½ quarts
Bulk	2¼ quarts	4½ quarts or 1¼ gallons	9 quarts or 2½ gallons
Beverages:			
Coffee	½ pound and 1½ gal. water	1 pound and 3 gal. water	2 pounds and 6 gal. water
Tea	1/12 pound and 1½ gal. water	⅙ pound and 3 gal. water	⅓ pound and 6 gal. water
Lemonade	10 to 15 lemons, 1½ gal. water	20 to 30 lemons, 3 gal. water	40 to 60 lemons, 6 gal. water

BREADS AND JELLIES

JANE'S PARKER HOUSE ROLLS

6 to 6½ c. flour	2 pkg. yeast
½ c. sugar	1 c. margarine
2 tsp. salt	1 egg

Combine 2½ cups flour and sugar, salt and yeast in large bowl. Add 1 cup margarine with mixer at low speed. Pour 2 cups hot water into this and add egg and increase speed to medium. Beat 2 minutes. Beat in ¾ cup flour and beat 2 more minutes. Spoon stir in 2½ to 3 cups flour to make soft dough. Knead 4 or 5 minutes and let rise 1½ hours. Punch down and let rest for 15 minutes, covered. In roasting pan, melt ½ cup butter. Roll out dough ½ inch thick. Cut with biscuit cutter. Dip in butter and fold over in half. Arrange in rows and let rise 40 minutes. Bake in 350° oven for 18 to 20 minutes.

RECIPE FOR LIFE

Good thoughts	Consideration for others
Kind deeds	Forgiveness

Mix all ingredients thoroughly. Add tears of joy, sorrow and sympathy for others. Fold in prayer and faith to lighten the other ingredients and raise the texture to great heights of Christian living. Bake well with the warmth of human kindness and serve with a smile!

PRIZE WINNING CINNAMON ROLLS

Several years ago, I shared some cinnamon rolls with a friend. She asked me for the recipe and sent it in and won the IGA Bake-Off contest. It has been printed on the IGA flour bag at Christmas time. The dough for the cinnamon rolls is the same recipe as the raised yeast doughnuts, Page 55. Following is the procedure for the cinnamon rolls.

Divide the dough in 2 parts. On floured surface, roll out one part at a time into a long roll, to ¾ inch thickness. Spread butter or margarine on dough, followed by sprinkling cinnamon over dough and then white sugar generously. Roll up, slicing to ¾ inch thick, with serrated edge knife, for easy slicing. Mix 1 cup brown sugar and 1 small carton whipping cream in pan which rolls are to be baked in. Place rolls on top. (If you want to make into all caramel rolls you will need to double ingredients.) If making plain cinnamon rolls, place rolls in greased pans. Let raise, covered with wax paper in warm area for 45 minutes. Bake in 350° oven until lightly browned.

Ice plain cinnamon rolls with confectioners icing, (p. 125). Place maraschino cherries and pecans on top to add beauty.

Note: Chopped nuts and cooked raisins are good added to the dough when dough is rolled out, but optional.

The best and most beautiful things in the world cannot be seen or touched but are felt in the heart.

DOUGHNUTS

These doughnuts are light and delicious!

2 c. warm water
3 env. yeast
3 eggs
1½ Tbsp. baking powder
⅓ c. sugar

¾ c. shortening or cooking oil
6 c. flour (approx.)
1½ tsp. salt
1½ tsp. vanilla

Dissolve yeast in ½ cup of the warm water. Add melted shortening or oil and sugar to rest of water. When cool, add eggs, baking powder, salt, vanilla and yeast mixture. Add enough flour to form soft dough. Let rise 20 minutes. Roll out ½ inch thick on floured board. Cut with doughnut cutter. Deep-fry until golden brown. Glaze: When cool, glaze with a mixture of icing sugar, hot water and vanilla flavoring.

BRAN ROLLS

You will enjoy making these delicious rolls. The recipe from a friend and country cook, Margaret Milhollin from Moberly, Mo.

5 c. plain flour
2 pkg dry yeast
¾ c. sugar
1 c. all bran cereal
1 c. crisco

2 eggs
1 t. salt
1 c. boiling water

Mix crisco, bran, sugar and 1 c. boiling water together. Set aside to cool. Put 1 c. lukewarm water with yeast in seperate bowl. Let stand 5 minutes. Beat eggs and mix with rest of ingredients with bran mixture, add yeast. Mix together real good. Knead well. Place in warm place for 1 hour or until double in size. Punch down and make into rolls and let rise. Bake in 400 degree oven 15 to 20 minutes. This dough can be refrigerated.

Gather the crumbs of happiness and they will make you a loaf of contentment.

RAISED YEAST DOUGHNUTS

Sharing my doughnut recipe over the years has been a joy. I have made dozens upon dozens for family, friends and for many special occasions. If directions are followed perfectly, anyone should have success in making them.

2 c. milk	2 eggs (room temperature)
1 stick margarine	2 pkg. dry yeast
½ c. sugar	7 c. flour
½ tsp. salt	

Scald milk, pour in large mixing bowl. Add margarine, sugar and salt, mixing well with mixer. When liquid is lukewarm, add yeast and mix well. Add eggs and mix well. Add 4 cups of the 7 cups flour, mixing well. Mix by hand the rest of the flour to make a very soft dough. Sometimes it might not take quite 7 cups flour. Pour out on lightly floured surface and knead for 6 minutes (5 with dough hook). Lightly grease dough and place in large bowl with lid, or cover with wax paper and cloth. Let rise in warm sun, warm water or by pilot light in gas oven, for 1½ to 2 hours or until double in bulk, very light to touch. Roll out dough to ¾ inch thick. Cut with doughnut cutter. Place in warm area on cloths or on racks in warm oven. Do not place doughnuts too close together. Cover, let rise until light, approximately 45 minutes. To fry, place doughnuts top down in medium hot oil. They will fry quickly. When medium brown, turn over to brown other side. Remove with fork and place on paper towels in a pan to drain off excess grease. Place in glaze and ice both sides.

Glaze:

1 box confectioners sugar	½ c. milk
½ stick margarine	1 tsp. vanilla

Heat milk and margarine and add to confectioners sugar. Blend ingredients together and add more milk if needed to make medium thick glaze. Add cinnamon to taste, to make cinnamon glaze.

CARAWAY PUFFS

1 pkg. dry yeast	1 tsp. salt
1⅓ c. flour	1 Tbsp. butter
¼ tsp. baking soda	1 egg
1 c. cream style cottage cheese	2 tsp. caraway seed
¼ c. water	2 Tbsp. grated onion
2 Tbsp. sugar	

In bowl, combine yeast, flour and baking soda. Heat together the cottage cheese and water, sugar, butter and salt until butter melts. Add dry ingredients. Add egg, caraway seed and grated onion. Beat on low speed for 1 minute and 3 minutes on high speed. Place in greased bowl, turning once. Cover; let rise till double in bulk (1½ hours). Divide among 12 well greased muffin pans. Cover, let rise, about 40 minutes. Bake in 400° oven about 15 minutes.

You cannot do a kindness too soon, because you never know how soon it will be too late.

ZUCCHINI BREAD
(Delicious! Always a treat.)

3 eggs, beaten
1 c. cooking oil
2 c. sugar
2 c. grated zucchini
2 tsp. vanilla

3 c. flour
1 tsp. soda
1 tsp. baking powder
1 tsp. salt
1 tsp. cinnamon

Preheat oven to 325°. Grease and flour 2 loaf pans; beat eggs, add oil, sugar, zucchini and vanilla. Sift and measure 3 cups flour. Sift with baking powder, soda, salt and cinnamon. Add to other ingredients. Mix thoroughly. Bake for 1 hour or until done.

Note: For a variety, add 1 cup crushed pineapple, 1 cup cooked raisins, drained, and 1 cup chopped pecans, or maybe not all three extras. Add ingredient to your liking. Delicious!

God, grant me the serenity to accept
The things I cannot change;
The courage to change the things I can,
And the wisdom to know the difference.

BRAN MUFFINS

First bowl: Pour **2 cups boiling water** over **2 cups 100% Bran Flakes.** Let stand.

Second bowl: Sift together **5 cups flour** and **5 teaspoons soda.**

Third bowl: Cream together:

1 c. shortening
3 c. sugar
4 eggs

1 qt. buttermilk
4 c. All-Bran

Combine all 3 mixtures. Bake at 350° for 20 minutes. Store in refrigerator up to 6 weeks.

Bread, the symbol of home and hospitality.

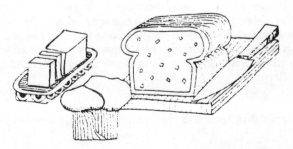

PLUCKIN BREAD

This Pluckin Bread was delivered to our door one morning by Doug Swanson, a coach from the high school, who was on his way to school. What a welcome surprise! I want to share this recipe with you. It is easy, good and would be fun for children to make.

4 tubes any kind canned biscuits,   **¾ c. sugar**
   cut each biscuit in 4 pieces   **1 tsp. cinnamon**

Shake or roll biscuits in this to keep from sticking togther. Place in angel food pan or Bundt pan that has been greased.

¾ c. butter   **½ tsp. cinnamon**
1 c. sugar

Boil and pour over pieces. Bake at 350° for 40 to 50 minutes. Let set 5 minutes in pan before removing.

SPOON CORN BREAD

2 c. milk   **1 Tbsp. melted shortening**
1 c. corn meal   **1 c. milk**
1 tsp. salt   **3 egg yolks, well beaten**
1 tsp. baking powder   **3 egg whites, stiffly beaten**

Cook corn meal in the milk until mush. Remove from stove. Add salt, baking powder, melted shortening, 1 cup milk and egg yolks. Fold in stiffly beaten egg whites. Bake in 2 quart greased baking dish for 1 hour at 350°.

ANGEL ROLLS

1 pkg. dry yeast   **½ c. sugar**
¼ c. warm water   **1 tsp. salt**
1 c. scalded milk   **½ c. cooking oil**
2 eggs   **4 c. unsifted flour**

Combine on night before dry yeast in warm water. Beat 2 eggs in large mixing bowl. Add sugar, salt and milk. Stir into mixture the dissolved yeast and oil. Add flour and stir. Let set covered overnight. You may hurry recipe by using 2 packages of yeast. Make in early morning and serve at noon. Next morning, put dough on floured board, turn over several times and divide into 2 parts. Do not work flour into dough. Roll each part round like a pie. Cut each into 16 wedges and roll up into roll (wide edge first). Place on greased pans or cookie sheets about 1½ inches apart. Let rise until light, bake 12 minutes at 375°. Great!

Give us this day our daily bread (Luke 11:3)

POTICA COFFEE CAKE

1 loaf frozen bread dough
½ c. brown sugar
¼ c. butter or oleo
1 egg

1 Tbsp. milk
1 Tbsp. orange rind
2 c. walnuts or pecans, chopped
Powdered sugar icing

Let well wrapped dough thaw out. Prepare filling by creaming brown sugar and butter. Then add egg, milk and orange rind. Stir in nuts and set aside. Roll dough in a 20x8 inch rectangle. Spread filling to within one inch of edges. Beginning from longest side, roll tightly in jelly roll fashion and pinch edges to seal. Place on greased baking sheet in a snail shaped coil. Cover; let rise until double in size. Bake at 375° for 30 to 40 minutes. Cool on wire rack. Frost with powdered sugar icing. Makes one large coffee cake.

IRISH SODA BREAD

This recipe is from the British Isles. Our church had a Missionary supper, with food fixed from different countries. Interesting dishes were prepared. I enjoyed making this bread and I really liked the flavor and texture.

4 c. unbleached flour
1 tsp. each soda, salt, cream of
    tartar
¾ c. sugar

3 oz. seedless raisins
¾ c. sugar
½ c. melted butter
1¾ c. buttermilk

Preheat oven to 375°. Sift dry ingredients into large bowl. Add butter, raisins and buttermilk. Mix to soft warm dough. Place dough on lightly floured surface and knead vigorously for 3 to 4 minutes, until dough is firm; then shape into 2 loaves. Moisten surface with buttermilk and dust with flour. Score the top with an X. Bake for 1 hour on a buttered and floured baking sheet until golden brown.

NO FUSS WHOLE WHEAT BREAD

Fresh bread in 1 hour from start to finish. Great rolls too.

7½ c. whole wheat flour
4 Tbsp. yeast
¼ c. honey

3½ c. warm water
1 Tbsp. salt
½ c. corn oil

Mix yeast and honey and with warm water. Add oil, salt and half of the flour. Mix and add rest of flour. Divide into 2 portions; put into oiled bread pans. Place in cold oven. Heat to 140° to raise 12 to 15 minutes. Turn oven to 375° and bake for 35 minutes. Makes 2 loaves.

Variation: For cinnamon bread, add 3 tablespoons cinnamon and 1 cup raisins with first addition of flour.

Lord, guide my willing hands
To bake my bread today,
To mix a little laughter
In what I do and say.

Let's all give thanks

BANANA BREAD

1½ c. sugar
¾ c. butter
2 eggs
2 very ripe bananas
2 c. flour

1 tsp. salt
½ c. buttermilk
1 tsp. vanilla
½ c. chopped nuts (optional)
1 tsp. soda

Cream sugar and butter; add eggs and mashed bananas. Sift together flour and soda; add to creamed mixture with buttermilk and vanilla. Bake in a loaf pan for 1 hour at 350

HONEY WHEAT BREAD

1 pkg. dry yeast
1 c. warm water
½ c. honey
1 tsp. salt

2 Tbsp. shortening
1 c. scalded milk
3 c. whole wheat flour
3 o. white flour

Dissolve yeast in warm water. Combine honey, salt, shortening, and hot milk; stir until shortening melts. Cool to lukewarm. Add yeast mixture. Gradually add flours. Knead until satiny, 8 to 10 minutes. Place in greased bowl; cover. Let rise in warm place for 2 to 2½ hours. Punch down; let rise again. Shape into 2 loaves. Put in greased pans, 9x5 inches. Let rise until tops of loaves are above pan edges. Bake at 350° for 50 to 60 minutes.

For freezer: Prepare same as the above. After shaping the loaves, place loaves in freezer loaf pans. Put in plastic bags and place in freezer. Then when you want to use them, take from freezer 6 hours before serving time, let rise and bake at 350° for 50 to 60 minutes.

Sprinkle caraway, poppy or sesame seed over dough which has been formed into desired shapes, brushed with butter.

CINNAMON ROLLS QUICK

I am happy that our daughter-in-laws enjoy cooking. Ruth Ann has Doug's approval with this recipe.

2½ c. lukewarm water
1 regular pkg. yellow or white cake
   mix

2 pkg. yeast
4½ c. flour

Dissolve yeast in water. Add cake mix and flour. Knead well. Let rise until double, about 2 hours. Roll ¼ inch thick and spread butter on dough, then sprinkle mixture of 1 cup brown sugar, 1 tablespoon cinnamon and ½ to 1 cup chopped nuts. Roll up and slice ½ inch thick. Place some brown sugar in bottom baking pan. Put in rolls. Bake at 350° for 25 to 30 minutes. Ice with confectioners icing (p. 125).

When bread is baking, a small dish of water in the oven will help to keep the crust from getting too hard.

*

MARY RUTH'S BUTTERHORNS

Unusual, easily made and you'll be surprised when you see the finished product.

Mix together:

2 soft sticks margarine

12 oz. small curd cottage cheese

Add:

2 c. flour

Dash of salt

Mix well and form into ball. Place in bowl, cover lightly. Refrigerate overnight (a must). Next day, divide into three balls. Roll out as for pie, on floured waxed paper. Cut in pie shaped wedges. Roll up from large end. Bake at 350° for 30 minutes. Drizzle confectioners icing on top (p. 125).

SUNDAY DINNER ROLLS

"Easy, excellent homemade rolls that even a beginner can excel in making."

2 eggs
⅔ c. sugar
1 pkg. yeast
1 c. warm water
½ c. cooking oil

¼ c. powdered milk
4 c. flour (approx.)
1 tsp. salt

Combine all ingredients except flour in large bowl and beat well with electric mixer. Add flour and salt and beat by hand until well mixed, this will be a sticky dough. Let stand overnight. The next morning, roll out in 2 large circles, using flour as needed. Cut pie shaped and roll. Place on greased cookie sheet. Let rise until after church. Bake at 375° for 12 to 15 minutes.

MILE-HIGH BISCUITS

A recipe from my friend Sharon Alison of Smyrna, Georgia, a gal who is very domestic. Sharon makes homemade bread every week. For a special treat try her homemade Biscuits soon.

3 cups all-purpose flour
2 Tbsp. sugar
1 Tbsp. plus 1½ teaspoons baking
  powder
¾ t. cream of tarter

¾ t. salt
¾ c. shortening
1 egg, beaten
¾ cup milk

Combine first 5 ingredients, mixing well; cut in shortening with a pastry blender until mixture resembles coarse meal. Combine egg and milk; add to flour mixture, stirring until dry ingredients are moistened. Turn dough out onto a lightly floured surface; knead 8 or 10 times.

Roll dough to 1-inch thickness; cut with a 2½-inch biscuit cutter. Place biscuits on an ungreased baking sheet. Bake at 450 for 15 minutes or until golden brown. Yield: 15 biscuits.

PERFECT SUNDAY DINNER ROLLS

"They will melt in your mouth and you just cannot fail."

1 pkg. dry yeast, dissolved in ¼ c.
warm water, plus 1 tsp. sugar
2 eggs
1 c. warm water

½ c. oil
1 tsp. salt
4 c. flour

Add sugar to yeast and water. Beat eggs in warm water and add oil and salt. Add to the yeast and sugar mixture. Gradually add flour. This dough is rather sticky and will rise at least twice its size, so use large bowl (it is not necessary to knead the dough). Let stand overnight and make out in morning by dividing the dough into about 4 parts. Be sure to use flour on the board or wax paper. Cut like a pizza and roll large end to small end and place on greased pans. Let stand ½ hour or until risen to light texture, then pop into the oven for 8 minutes at 375°.

My mom's the finest cook on earth
And she told me long ago,
That bread's no good unless you add
Some lovin to the dough.

RECIPE FOR A HAPPY FAMILY

1 husband
1 wife, children (several)
1 home
1 Bible for each
Generous portion of prayer
3 cups of love, packed
1 package of work

1 package of play, together
1 tablespoon of patience
1 tablespoon understanding
1 tablespoon of forgiveness
1 small paddle
1 cup kisses

Mix thoroughly and sprinkle with awareness. Bake in moderate oven of everyday life, using as fuel all the grudges and past unpleasantness. Cool. Turn out onto platter of cheerfulness. Garnish with tears and laughter. And in large helpings, serve God, country and community.

CROCK POT APPLE BUTTER

Cook apples and make sauce. Use 1 cup applesauce, ½ cup sugar, 1 teaspoon cinnamon, and ½ teaspoon cloves. Mix together and pour in crock pot. Crock pot will hold about 8 cups. Cover and cook on HIGH 8 to 10 hours. Remove lid during last half of time. Stir occasionally. Pour into sterilized jars and seal.

One man with courage makes a majority.

RHUBARB JAM

...rb, cubed
...ugar

1 small can crushed pineapple
1 small box cherry Jello

Mix the rhubarb and sugar and let stand for 2½ hours. Cook 10 minutes. Add pineapple. Cook 7 minutes longer. Remove from stove. Add Jello. Yields 5 jars.

RHUBARB STRAWBERRY JAM

4 c. rhubarb, chopped
3½ c. sugar

¼ c. water
1 pkg. strawberry Jello

Cook rhubarb, sugar and water for 15 minutes on medium hot heat, boiling. Add strawberry Jello and mix well with the above. Makes 2 pints. Can be stored in refrigerator for a long time. Very good.

APRICOT JAM
(Zucchini style)

Super good! Tastes like peach jam.

6 c. grated and peeled zucchini
5 c. sugar
½ c. lemon juice

1 large can crushed pineapple (do not drain)
6 oz. pkg. apricot Jello

Boil zucchini and sugar 15 minutes. Add lemon juice and pineapple. Boil 10 minutes more. Stir in Jello. Mix well. Pour into sterile jars and seal. Either keep in refrigerator or you can freeze it.

STRAWBERRY PRESERVES

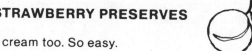

Delicious over ice cream too. So easy.

1 C. berries

1 c. sugar

Bring to a boil and boil for 10 minutes, stirring constantly. Skim top when necessary. Add another cup berries and another cup sugar. Bring to a boil again and cook 10 minutes. Pour into a large bowl and let cool. Spoon into containers and freeze.

When making jam, rub the bottom of the pan with butter. This prevents burning and keeps the jam clear.

"One who uses the Bible as his guide never loses his sense of Direction."

Desserts, Cakes, Pies and Pastries

HANDY CHART OF KITCHEN MATH
(Size of Pans and Baking Dishes)

Cooking need never become a crisis, when you use our handy charts. Need a 4 or 6-cup baking dish?
Will your fancy mold be the right size for the recipe? See below for the answers.

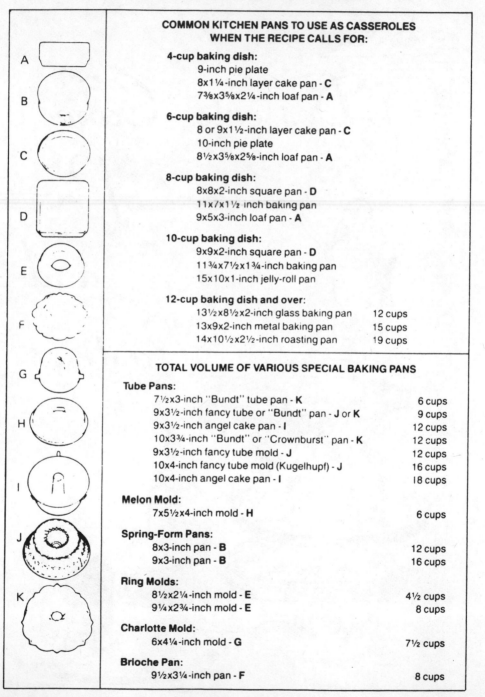

COMMON KITCHEN PANS TO USE AS CASSEROLES WHEN THE RECIPE CALLS FOR:

4-cup baking dish:
- 9-inch pie plate
- 8x1¼-inch layer cake pan - **C**
- 7⅜x3⅝x2¼-inch loaf pan - **A**

6-cup baking dish:
- 8 or 9x1½-inch layer cake pan - **C**
- 10-inch pie plate
- 8½x3⅝x2⅝-inch loaf pan - **A**

8-cup baking dish:
- 8x8x2-inch square pan - **D**
- 11x7x1½ inch baking pan
- 9x5x3-inch loaf pan - **A**

10-cup baking dish:
- 9x9x2-inch square pan - **D**
- 11¾x7½x1¾-inch baking pan
- 15x10x1-inch jelly-roll pan

12-cup baking dish and over:
- 13½x8½x2-inch glass baking pan   12 cups
- 13x9x2-inch metal baking pan   15 cups
- 14x10½x2½-inch roasting pan   19 cups

TOTAL VOLUME OF VARIOUS SPECIAL BAKING PANS

Tube Pans:
7½x3-inch "Bundt" tube pan - **K**	6 cups
9x3½-inch fancy tube or "Bundt" pan - **J** or **K**	9 cups
9x3½-inch angel cake pan - **I**	12 cups
10x3¾-inch "Bundt" or "Crownburst" pan - **K**	12 cups
9x3½-inch fancy tube mold - **J**	12 cups
10x4-inch fancy tube mold (Kugelhupf) - **J**	16 cups
10x4-inch angel cake pan - **I**	18 cups

Melon Mold:
7x5½x4-inch mold - **H**	6 cups

Spring-Form Pans:
8x3-inch pan - **B**	12 cups
9x3-inch pan - **B**	16 cups

Ring Molds:
8½x2¼-inch mold - **E**	4½ cups
9¼x2¾-inch mold - **E**	8 cups

Charlotte Mold:
6x4¼-inch mold - **G**	7½ cups

Brioche Pan:
9½x3¼-inch pan - **F**	8 cups

DESSERTS, CAKES, PIES AND PASTRIES

JUST LIKE MOTHER

He criticized her pudding, he
didn't like her cake;
He wished she'd make the biscuits
his mother used to make.
She didn't wash the dishes, and
she didn't make a stew;
And she didn't darn his socks like
his mother used to do.
And then one day he went the same
"old ritual" through;
She turned and boxed his ears--just
like his mother used to do.

CREAM PUFFS

Can be made several days in advance and filled shortly before serving. A delightful dessert!

1 c. water	1 c. sifted flour
½ c. butter or margarine	4 eggs

Combine water and butter in a medium saucepan and heat to boiling. Stir in flour all at once. Stir mixture vigorously over low heat until mixture leaves the sides of pan and forms a ball. Remove from heat. Beat in eggs 1 at a time. Beat mixture until it is smooth and velvety. Drop from a tablespoon onto ungreased baking sheet (allow 2 inches between dough). Bake for 10 minutes in 450° oven, then 25 minutes at 350°. Fill with a pudding filling, sprinkle with powdered sugar.

Variation: Bake miniature cream puffs and stuff with ham or tuna salad or cream cheese mixtures.

BAKED CUSTARD

I'll rate this number 1 for the best custard I've tasted.

6 slightly beaten eggs	2 tsp. vanilla
½ c. sugar	½ tsp. salt
4 c. milk, scalded	⅓ c. brown sugar
½ tsp. nutmeg	

Combine eggs, sugar and salt. Slowly stir in hot milk and vanilla. Coat bottom and sides of baking dish with melted brown sugar. Pour custard mixture into dish and bake in 325° oven in a pan of hot water. Bake 50 to 60 minutes or until knife inserted in center comes out clean.

The dandelion is a thing which,
If given an inch, will take a yard.

 Happiness makes up in height what it lacks in length.

79

ICE CREAM DESSERT

Greg is a youth minister. Patty, our daughter-in-law, shared this recipe with me because it has been so successful entertaining the teens.

2 c. crushed Rice Krispies cereal
1 c. shredded coconut
½ c. chopped pecans

¾ c. brown sugar
½ c. melted butter
½ gal. vanilla ice cream

Mix the first 5 ingredients together. Put ⅔ of mixture in bottom of 9x13 inch pan. Pour in softened ice cream and spread. Put the rest of the mixture on top. Put in freezer to harden.

BAKED LEMON PUDDING

If you like the flavor of lemon, you will enjoy this change. I remember Mother serving this many times through the years.

3 Tbsp. butter
1⅛ c. sugar
Juice of 1½ lemons
Grated rind of 1 lemon

1½ c. milk
3 Tbsp. flour
3 eggs, separated

Cream butter and sugar together. Add beaten egg yolks, flour, lemon juice and rind. Mix thoroughly, add milk, fold in stiffly beaten egg whites. Pour into individual baking dishes. Bake in pan with water in bottom, in 350° oven for 35 to 40 minutes.

One thing is always sure to please,
Just give them pudding such as these.

A QUICK DESSERT

Aunt Agnes has a great sense of humor. She is a retired nurse now and lives in Prescott, Ar. Cooking is not one of her favorite past-times, but she has come up with some easy, good recipes. After enjoying a good laugh, decided to share it with you. The recipe reads like this:

And then for the busy housewife who hasn't done a thing all day, but lay around and suddenly realizes it is time for her husband to be home, this is a delightful quicky for dessert - I always use this for dessert for a dinner - because it is a sure thing, no errors can be made - and then you haven't exhausted yourself trying to think of a dessert - and all ingredients are easily picked up at the shopping district----

Angel food cake
Whipped cream

Top with frozen fruit of any kind

A merry heart doeth good like a medicine - Proverbs 17:22

BUTTERSCOTCH TORTE
(Four layers)

1 c. flour
1 c. chopped pecans
1 stick margarine, melted
1 (8 oz.) pkg. cream cheese, softened
1 c. Cool Whip (or other whipped topping)

1 c. confectioners sugar
2 pkg. butterscotch pudding (instant may be used)
1 large container Cool Whip (or other whipped topping)
½ c. chopped pecans or Heath brickle chips (optional)

Mix flour, pecans, and margarine. Spread in 9x13 inch pan. Bake for 20 minutes in 350° oven. Cool. Mix cream cheese, 1 cup Cool Whip and confectioners sugar until creamy. Spread over baked layer. Prepare pudding, using only 3 cups milk. Cool and spread over second layer. Top with Cool Whip and sprinkle with chopped pecans or Heath brickle chips.

Variation: Use chocolate pudding and sprinkle chocolate Hershey's bar shavings. Lemon pudding can be used. Or, try a vanilla pudding with coconut on top. Color the coconut for the holidays.

YOU'RE LUCKY IF THERE'S ANY LEFT DESSERT

You might enjoy making this to serve at a family dinner or pot luck, or will keep well refrigerated for a couple of days. Guaranteed to disappear quickly.

2 c. flour
2 c. chopped pecans

2 sticks melted butter

Mix crust well and press into a long cake pan. Bake at 250° oven for 20 minutes.

First Filling:

1 (8 oz.) container Cool Whip, thawed
1 (8 oz.) bar Philadelphia cream cheese

1 c. confectioners sugar

Mix filling well and spread on top of cooled crust.

Second Crust:

4½ c. milk

3 pkg. chocolate instant pudding

Mix filling well and spread on top of cheese filling and chill 15 minutes. Sprinkle top with pecans.

Note: Lemon pudding might be your favorite.

SOUTHERN RICE PUDDING

3 eggs (slightly beaten)
½ c. sugar
¼ t. salt
1 c. cooked rice

2 ⅓ c. milk
1 t. vanilla
1 t. lemon
Raisins if desired (½ c.)

Mix together and bake at 350 degrees about ½ hr. Use a little more sugar for a sweeter pudding.

OREO COOKIE DESSERT

Crust: Crumble one large package of Oreo cookies, saving enough dry crumbs to sprinkle on top of finished dessert. Add 1 stick of soft butter, mix thoroughly and pat into 9x13 inch pan.

Filling: Mix one large box of instant vanilla pudding with 2¾ cups milk. Add 1 carton Cool Whip and 8 ounces cream cheese. Mix well. Pour on crust and top with cookie crumbs. Refrigerate.

REAL CHEESE CAKE

Delicious. Tastes like homemade ice cream.

For crust: Take 1¾ cups graham cracker crumbs, ¼ cup finely chopped English walnuts or pecans, ½ teaspoon cinnamon and ½ cup melted butter, mixing well and press into a 9 inch springform pan. Press up sides a bit.

Filling: Beat until smooth 3 eggs, 2 (8 ounce) softened packages cream cheese, 1 cup sugar, ¼ teaspoon salt, 2 teaspoons vanilla, and 1 teaspoon lemon or almond extract. Beat until smooth. Blend in 3 cups sour cream. Pour in crust. Bake in 350° oven for 35 minutes. Refrigerate 4 to 5 hours.

LITTLE CHEESE CAKES

Very good, quick to make and children love them. We have two sons that married sisters, Missouri farm girls. Brenda and Ruth Ann enjoy making "goodies" such as these, for Tim and Doug and share their cooking talents with friends and relatives too!!

2 (8 oz.) pkg. cream cheese
¾ c. sugar
2 eggs

1 tsp. vanilla
Vanilla wafers

Use cupcake papers in cupcake pans. Lay one vanilla wafer in each, flat side down. Mix rest of ingredients together. Fill each not quite half full to make 24 little cakes. Bake at 375° for 15 minutes. Cool completely. Top with cherry pie filling. Chill and store in refrigerator. Take out of papers by pulling papers away.

SEVEN UP CAKE

Yum Yum good, Company cake. The recipe from an excellent cook and a friend Bertie Land, of Dannville, Illinois.

1 box Duncan Hines Lemon
    Supreme cake mix
1 box pineapple instant
    pudding mix

4 eggs
¾ c. wesson oil
1 (10oz.) can or
    1 bottle 7-up

Bake in a 375 degree oven about 40 miutes in a 9 x 13 pan.

The joy of the Lord is my strength. (Nehemiah 8:10)

RASPBERRY DELIGHT

A delicious dessert that never fails to rate compliments. Serve with a scoop of ice cream.

½ c. margarine
2 egg yolks
1 c. sugar
1 tsp. vanilla
2 Tbsp. cornstarch
1 pt. frozen raspberries

1 ¼ c. flour
¼ tsp. soda
¼ tsp. salt
4 Tbsp. chopped walnuts
2 egg whites

Beat margarine and egg yolks with ⅓ cup sugar until light and fluffy. Add vanilla and sifted flour, soda and salt. Spread in ungreased pan. Combine ¼ cup sugar, cornstarch and raspberries. Cook until thick. Spread this over uncooked mixture. Sprinkle 2 tablespoons nuts over this. Beat egg whites, gradually add 1 tablespoon sugar and spread over above mixture. Sprinkle with nuts. Stand in pan of water and bake at 350° for 30 minutes.

CARAMEL ICE CREAM DELIGHT
(Melts in your mouth!)

2 c. chopped pecans
1 c. flour
½ c. margarine

½ gal. butter brickle ice cream
1 (8 to 10 oz.) jar caramel sauce

Mix 1 cup pecans, flour and margarine together and press into 1 (9x13 inch) baking dish. Bake at 350° for 25 minutes. When crust is completely cooled, slice half of the ice cream in half inch slices and place on crust. Drizzle half of the caramel sauce over ice cream and sprinkle ½ cup pecans over the sauce. Repeat. Place in freezer. Serves 12.

PERFECT BREAD PUDDING

Something different. A similar recipe is served in restaurants. Rosalie McClard, who lives in Alpharetta, Georgia, is a former High School Teacher, at one time, represented St. Louis, Mo, in the Rose Bowl parade. She classes herself as a spur of the moment cook. Rosalie enjoys entertaining friends.

2 ¼ c. milk
2 eggs, slightly beaten
½ brown sugar
2 c. day old bread cubes
½ t. cinnamon

1 t. vanilla
¼ t. salt
½ c. seedless raisins

Combine milk and eggs and pour over bread cubes. Stir in remaining ingredients. Pour into 8 inch baking dish.

SAUCE FOR BREAD PUDDING

Mix ½ sugar, 2 t. cornstarch and ½ t. nutmeg. Gradually stir in 1 c. water. Cook over low heat until thick and clear. Stir small amount of mixture into beaten egg yolks. Return to hot mixture. Cook and stir 1 minute. Remove from heat and add 2 T. butter or margarine, ½ t. grated lemon peel and 2 T. lemon juice. Blend thoroughly. Serve warm.

PUMPKIN ROLL

Our daughter-in-law Brenda, enjoys making this and Tim enjoys eating it!

3 eggs
1 c. sugar
⅔ c. pumpkin
1 tsp. lemon juice
¾ c. flour
1 tsp. baking powder

2 tsp. cinnamon
1 tsp. ginger
½ tsp. nutmeg
½ tsp. salt
1 c. nuts (optional)
Powdered sugar

Beat eggs on high speed for 5 minutes. Add sugar to eggs. Stir the pumpkin and lemon juice into egg mixture. Stir together all the remaining ingredients except the nuts and powdered sugar. Fold into the pumpkin mixture and mix. Bake at 375° for 15 minutes in small cookie sheet or 15x10x1 inch pan. Turn out on towel sprinkled with powdered sugar. Roll towel and cake together. Cool. Unroll and spread with filling. Roll the cake again and chill.

Filling:

4 Tbsp. soft butter
2 to 3 oz. cream cheese, beaten

1 c. powdered sugar
1 tsp. vanilla

Combine all ingredients and beat until smooth and spread on roll.

BANANA SPLIT CAKE
(A delicious dessert)

2 c. graham cracker crumbs

1 stick margarine, melted

Press the above mixture in 9x13 inch pan. Whip below mixture for at least 15 minutes and spread over the crumb crust:

2 c. powdered sugar
2 sticks cold margarine

2 eggs

Then layer:

5 sliced bananas
1 small can crushed pineapple,
    drained
1 can strawberry pie filling

1 large ctn. Cool Whip
Chopped nuts
Halved maraschino cherries
    (optional)

Refrigerate and serve with ice cream.

NEVER FAIL CHOCOLATE DEVILS FOOD CAKE

½ c. cocoa
2 tsp. soda
½ c. cold water
¾ c. butter or margarine
1 ¾ c. sugar
2 egg yolks

¾ c. Sour Milk or cream
1 t. vanilla
2 ½ c. flour
1 t. salt
2 egg whites, beaten

Mix well, the cocoa, water and soda. Let stand while rest of cake is measured. Cream butter, sugar and yolks, vanilla. Blend well. Add cocoa mixture and blend. Put salt in flour and add alternately with sour milk and vanilla mixture. Fold in beaten egg whites. Bake in greased round pans or 9 x 13 pan. Bake in 350 degree oven for 30 - 35 minutes. Cool on rack, top side up.

FUDGE CUPCAKES

You must try this recipe, great for picnics or anytime. Requires no icing, tastes like brownies, fun to make and just stir up in a bowl.

4 sq. semi-sweet chocolate	**1 tsp. vanilla**
2 sticks butter	**4 eggs**
1½ c. chopped pecans	**¼ tsp. burnt sugar flavoring**
1¾ c. sugar	**(optional)**
1 c. flour	

Melt butter and chocolate in a heavy pan. Add nuts and stir until coated. Let cool. Combine sugar and flour. Add beaten eggs and vanilla. Last, add butter and chocolate mixture. Mix well, but do not beat. Bake in greased muffin tins for 35 minutes at 325°.

Note: Cupcake liners can be used, preferably the Reynolds Wrap ones.

FRUIT CAKE

The best fruit cake I've tried. Can be baked a few days before the holidays. Wrap tightly and it will keep well refrigerated.

1 c. butter	**¾ c. buttermilk**
2 c. sugar	**8 oz. pkg. dates, cut up**
5 eggs	**1 lb. orange candy slices, cut in**
1 Tbsp. vanilla	**small pieces**
4 c. sifted flour	**4 oz. can Angel Flake coconut**
½ tsp. soda	**2 c. pecans**
1 tsp. salt	

Cut orange slices in small pieces. (They cut easier if you leave them in the refrigerator to get hard.) In bowl, combine candy, dates, nuts and coconut and dredge with ¼ cup of the 4 cups flour and set aside. Sift rest of flour with soda and salt. Cream butter and sugar until fluffy. Add eggs, one at a time, add vanilla, mixing well. Add dry ingredients alternately with buttermilk. Fold in date and candy mixture. Pour into a well greased tube pan. Bake at 300° for 2½ hours. Or, cook cake in 2 loaf pans, decreasing baking time 20 minutes.

Glaze:

Grated peel from 1 lemon, 1 orange	**¼ c. lemon juice**
or 1 tsp. of each	**¼ c. orange juice**

Mix with ½ cup of powdered sugar and pour over hot cake. Let cool in pan. Remove from pan.

Note: Freezes beautifully.

"Gather the crumbs of happiness and they will make you a loaf of contentment."

BUTTERMILK PINEAPPLE CARROT CAKE

The buttermilk, pineapple and coconut make it super moist!

2 c. flour
1½ c. sugar
1 tsp. cinnamon
2 tsp. baking soda
¾ c. buttermilk
1 (8½ oz.) can crushed pineapple
½ c. oil

3 eggs
2 tsp. vanilla
½ tsp. salt
1 c. coconut
1 c. chopped walnuts
2 c. grated carrots

Combine dry ingredients; blend in oil, eggs and buttermilk. Add remaining ingredients; mix well. Bake at 350° for 45 minutes. Frost with Cream Cheese Frosting (p. 94).

Frostings, fillings, icings and glaze,
Use them freely - the results will amaze.

CREAM OF COCONUT CAKE
(Delicious!)

¼ c. Crisco oil
2 eggs
½ c. nut pieces
1 c. coconut

1½ c. water
1 white cake mix (plus pudding -
    super moist - sour cream)

Mix this all well together - beating for 2 minutes at medium speed. Bake at 350° for 30 to 40 minutes. With cake warm, put holes in top of it with a large fork or can use a small wooden spoon handle. Pour 1 can of cream of coconut over top of cake. Let cool.

Topping:

8 oz. Cool Whip
1 c. coconut

½ c. fine chopped nut pieces

Mix well together and spread evenly over cooked cake. Keep refrigerated.

WALDORF ASTORIA CAKE
(Red Velvet Cake)

Cooking and baking can be an exciting experience! This cake is beautiful to serve at Christmas, New Years, Valentine's day or just an ordinary day. Our sons have requested it for a Birthday cake.

1½ cups sugar
½ cup crisco
¼ cup Puritan oil
2 eggs
1½ ounces red food coloring
2 tablespoons cocoa
2½ cups sifted cake flour

1 cup buttermilk
1 tsp. salt
1 tsp. soda
1 tsp. baking powder
1 tsp. vinegar

Sift together the flour, cocoa, baking powder and salt. Cream crisco, oil, sugar and eggs, beating well. Add food coloring. Alternately add cake flour and buttermilk. Mix well. Add baking soda and vinegar, blending in well. Bake in 3 layer cake pans at 350 degrees for 25 minutes. (or cookie sheet or 9 by 13 inch pan. Use tooth pick test as time will vary)

Frosting:
¾ cup milk
4 tbsp. flour
⅓ c. softened margarine
⅓ c. crisco

pinch salt
¾ c. sugar
1 tsp. vanilla

Cook milk and flour until thick. Cool. Cream together butter, sugar and vanilla. Add to cooled mixture. Beat until fluffy, about 3 minutes.

OVERNIGHT COFFEE CAKE

2 c. flour
1 tsp. baking powder
1 tsp. soda
1 tsp. cinnamon
½ tsp. salt
⅔ c. butter
1 c. sugar

½ c. brown sugar
2 eggs
1 c. buttermilk
½ c. brown sugar
½ c. chopped walnuts
1 tsp. cinnamon
¼ tsp. nutmeg

Sift flour, baking powder, soda, salt and cinnamon. Cream butter and sugar with ½ cup brown sugar. Add eggs. Add dry ingredients with buttermilk. Spread in greased and floured 9x13 inch pan. Combine ½ cup brown sugar, nuts, ½ teaspoon cinnamon and ½ teaspoon nutmeg. Sprinkle over batter. Refrigerate overnight. Bake at 350° for 45 minutes.

A toothpick inserted, and comes out clean shows your cake is done.

Tim and Brenda

BUTTERMILK POUND CAKE

I have enjoyed baking and decorating our childrens wedding cakes. I have used this recipe that I wish to share with you. Of course I had to make several recipes to produce the cake. It was fun!

Large recipe - Sift together:

5 c. flour	**1 tsp. soda**
2 tsp. salt	**3⅓ c. sugar**
4 tsp. baking powder	

Add:

2 c. buttermilk	**2 tsp. lemon flavoring**
1½ c. Crisco	**½ tsp. butter flavoring**
2 tsp. vanilla	**8 egg whites**

Half recipe - Sift together:

2½ c. flour	**½ tsp. soda**
1 tsp. salt	**1⅔ c. sugar**
1 tsp. baking soda	

Add:

1 c. buttermilk	**1½ tsp. lemon flavoring**
¾ c. Crisco	**¼ tsp. butter flavoring**
1 tsp. vanilla	**4 egg whites**

Beat for 2 minutes or until light and fluffy. Add egg whites. Beat two more minutes or until all egg whites are incorporated into the batter. Bake in 350° oven in greased, waxed paper lined pans until very light brown or the toothpick test.

Doug and Ruth Ann

WEDDING CAKE ICING

Very easy to prepare, I have received numerous compliments with this icing. A good icing for all occasion cakes. Double or triple recipe as needed for large cake.

1 lb. confectioners sugar	1 tsp. vanilla
½ c. whole milk	4 tsp. butter flavoring or 4 drops of
⅔ c. Crisco	Wilton butter flavoring

With mixer, blend the confectioners sugar and Crisco together. Gradually add milk and flavorings, beating well to creamy spreading consistency. A little extra milk may be needed. The real buttery flavor really makes this cake good, so depending on the brand used, more might be necessary. This is important to make an excellent icing for this type cake.

DECORATOR ICING

To decorate a wedding cake or special occasion cake.

1 lb. confectioners sugar	1 tsp. vanilla
⅓ c. milk	3 tsp. butter flavoring or 3 drops
1 c. Crisco	Wilton butter flavoring

Blend confectioners sugar and Crisco together, adding milk and flavorings to make stiff icing consistency for decorating. Divide icing and make colors needed.

It is easier to fight for ones's principles than to live up to them.

Smiles are like the sunshine
They freshen up our day;
They bring happiness to life
And drive our cares away!

NEVER FAIL SEVEN MINUTE FROSTING
(A delicious frosting for your favorite cake!!)

3 egg whites (room temperature)   1 Tbsp. water
¾ c. sugar   1 tsp. vanilla
¾ c. light Karo syrup

Put all ingredients in top of double over cold water. Turn on stove to medium high heat. Beat continuously with electric beater until frosting stands in peaks, approximately 7 minutes. Spread on cake.

RAINBOW CAKE

You'll love its moist, fruity taste. What a colorful way to end a meal.

1 pkg. white cake mix or pudding   ½ c. cold water
   included cake mix   2 c. thawed whipped topping
1 (3 oz.) pkg. strawberry Jello   1 box vanilla instant pudding
1 c. boiling water

A. Prepare cake mix as directed on package, baking in well greased and floured 13x9 inch pan. Cool cake in pan 15 minutes. Then prick with utility fork at ½ inch intervals.

B. Meanwhile, dissolve gelatin in boiling water. Add cold water and carefully pour over warm cake. Chill 3 to 4 hours.

C. In a chilled, deep bowl, blend and whip topping mix, instant pudding, and cold milk until stiff, 3 to 8 minutes. Frost cake and store in refrigerator.

It takes both sunshine and rain to make a rainbow.

CHOCOLATE CAKE

A favorite recipe from my friend Marie Bagby, from Huntsville, Missouri. Moist and delicious!

Cream together ½ cup margarine, 2 cups sugar and 2 eggs. Add to the above ½ cup sour milk, and the sifted 2 cups flour, 1 teaspoon salt, 2 teaspoons soda and ½ cup cocoa. Add 1 cup boiling water, then 1 teaspoon vanilla. Bake in 9x13 inch cake pan at 350° for 30 minutes or until done.

Gossip is like a balloon—It grows bigger with every puff.

MISSISSIPPI MUD CAKE

½ c. butter, softened
1 c. sugar
3 eggs
¾ c. all-purpose flour
½ tsp. baking powder
Dash of salt

¼ c. plus 1½ Tbsp. cocoa
1 tsp. vanilla extract
1 c. chopped pecans
1 (10 oz.) pkg. marshmallows
Chocolate Frosting

Cream butter; gradually add sugar, beating well. Add eggs, one at a time, beating well after each addition. Combine flour, baking powder, salt and cocoa; add to creamed mixture. Stir in vanilla and pecans. Spoon batter into a greased 13x9x2 inch glass baking pan. Bake at 325° for 15 to 18 minutes or until top is barely soft to the touch. Remove cake from oven and cover top with marshmallows. Return to oven for 2 minutes or until marshmallows are soft. Spread marshmallows over cake and immediately cover with Chocolate Frosting. Let frosting harden before cutting the cake into squares.

Chocolate Frosting:

¼ c. butter or margarine
¼ c. plus 2 Tbsp. cocoa
¼ c. plus 3 Tbsp. warm milk

1 tsp. vanilla extract
1 (16 oz.) pkg. confectioners sugar

Cream butter; add cocoa mixing well. Gradually beat in confectioners sugar adding warm milk as necessary, until spreading consistency. Stir in vanilla. Spread immediately over warm marshmallows. Enough icing for 1 (13x9 inch) cake.

MISSISSIPPI MUD

You'll enjoy this moist cake, the recipe from our niece Mary Remole, who lives in Potomac, Il., a gal who enjoys cooking.

½ c. butter
⅔ c. sugar
4 eggs
1 tsp. vanilla
¾ c. flour

2 Tbsp. cocoa
¼ tsp. baking powder
¼ tsp. salt
Marshmallows

Put in bottom of greased 9x13 inch pan. Bake in 350° oven for 15 minutes. Remove from oven. Sprinkle the above with marshmallows and bake 3 minutes. Allow to cool.

Icing:

1 (6 oz.) pkg. chocolate bits
1 c. peanut butter

1½ c. Rice Krispies

Cook chocolate bits and peanut butter over low heat until chocolate is melted. Pour in Rice Krispies and pour over cake.

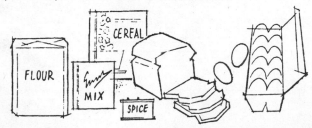

CARROT CAKE

When we had our restaurant, this cake became very popular. One fellow came in one day before it was iced. He waited while I made the icing and he took 4 pieces with him. I did not use the nuts or raisins. Some people do not care for raisins and the "popular demand" seemed to be without nuts. I'm happy to share this recipe with you!

2 c. flour	3 tsp. cinnamon
2 c. sugar	1½ c. Wesson oil
2 tsp. soda	3 c. grated carrots
1 tsp. salt	4 eggs

Sift dry ingredients together and set aside. In mixing bowl, cream sugar, eggs and oil together. Add carrots and mix. Add dry ingredients and mix well, but not over-beating. Bake in 9x13 inch pan for 35 minutes. Use the toothpick test, as some ovens vary. Use Cream Cheese Icing.

Cream Cheese Icing:

1 (8 oz.) pkg. cream cheese	1 lb. box confectioners sugar
½ stick butter	2 tsp. vanilla

Cream cheese with butter until smooth. Add confectioners sugar and vanilla and beat well. Enough icing for a large cake.

Note: If icing makes more than you want for a particular cake, try using it between graham crackers. Children love them. And big kids too!

APPLE DAPPLE CAKE
(A moist cake, simple, yet impressive.)

3 eggs	1 tsp. soda
2 c. sugar	1 tsp. cinnamon
1½ c. oil	½ c. nuts, chopped
3 c. flour	1 c. raisins (optional)
2 tsp. vanilla	3 c. apples
1 tsp. salt	

Mix the eggs, oil and sugar together. Add the dry ingredients and vanilla. Add the nuts, apples and raisins and mix well. Bake in greased 9x13 inch pan for 45 minutes.

Topping:

1 stick margarine	¼ tsp. vanilla
1 c. brown sugar	½ c. nuts, chopped
¼ c. milk	¼ tsp. cloves (optional)

Combine margarine, brown sugar, milk, cloves and vanilla. Boil for 5 minutes. Pour over cake while hot. Sprinkle with nuts.

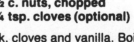

For black frosting for party cupcakes, add blue food coloring to your favorite chocolate frosting.

When separating an egg, if a bit of yolk gets into the whites, remove with a piece of egg shell.

If you keep candles for the birthday cake in the refrigerator for a day before using, they will burn slowly and evenly.

"Remember, there is blue sky behind the blackest cloud."

HAPPY BIRTHDAY CAKE

Do you know anyone who likes to make all her cakes from "scratch?" I've never known my sister-in-law Geneva, to do any different. She has that reputation and has shared this recipe with me that I know you will enjoy.

⅔ c. Crisco	1 tsp. salt
1⅔ c. sugar	3½ tsp. baking powder
3 eggs	½ c. milk
2½ c. flour	1 tsp. vanilla

Cream sugar and Crisco well. Add eggs; beat again. Add dry ingredients that have been sifted together. Blend by mixer 2 minutes. Pour into 2 (9 inch) round layer cake pans, greased with Crisco and lined with waxed paper. Bake at 375° for 30 to 35 minutes, or when toothpick is inserted in cake comes out clean.

Icing for Birthday Cake:

2 Tbsp. water	1 egg
4½ Tbsp. sugar	⅔ c. Crisco
2½ c. confectioners sugar	1 tsp. vanilla

Boil water and sugar one minute. Cool. Beat confectioners sugar with egg. Combine 2 mixtures. Add Crisco, vanilla, beating until creamy. Remove ⅓ cup icing. Tint with a few drops of green or yellow coloring. Spread white icing between layers, on sides and top of cake. With a knife or pastry tube place five lines of icing ½ inch apart to make scale. Use candied cherries for notes.

"Never complain about birthdays. Those that have birthdays live the longest."

CARAMEL FROSTING

1½ c. brown sugar
¾ c. cream or milk

2 Tbsp. butter
½ tsp. vanilla

Cook sugar with cream or milk until it forms a soft ball when dropped in cold water (about ½ hour), add butter and vanilla. Remove from fire and beat until right consistency to spread.

For by grace are ye saved through faith; and that not of yourselves: It is the gift of God. Ephesians 2:8

RECIPE FOR HAPPINESS

Use:

2 heaping cups of patience
1 heartful of love
2 handfuls of generosity

1 dash of laughter
1 headful of understanding

Sprinkle generously with kindness and add plenty of faith and mix well. Spread over a period of a lifetime and serve to everyone you meet.

ITALIAN CREAM CAKE

This cake is often served in restaurants and is a delicious moist cake that will rate high with you. Any occasion cake. Good for the holidays. We attended a wedding in which this cake was served. It keeps very well. Frost with Cream Cheese Frosting.

1 stick oleo
½ c. Crisco
1¾ c. sugar
5 egg yolks
2 c. flour
1 tsp. soda
½ tsp. salt

1 tsp. vanilla
1 c. buttermilk
1 c. Angel Flake coconut
1 c. chopped pecans or English
        walnuts
5 egg whites, stiffly beaten

Cream the first 3 ingredients; add egg yolks and beat well. Add sifted dry ingredients and buttermilk. Stir in coconut, nuts and vanilla. Fold in egg whites, stiffly beaten. Pour batter into 3 greased and floured 9 inch cake pans. Bake at 350° for 25 minutes.

Note: Chopped pecans or walnuts add a special touch to the top of the cake.

CREAM CHEESE FROSTING

1 (8 oz.) pkg. cream cheese
1 box confectioner's sugar

½ stick butter
2 teaspoons vanilla

Beat together the cream cheese and butter. Add confectioner's sugar and vanilla and beat until smooth.
Note: Garnish with nut halves on top.

FUDGE FROSTING OR FUDGE?

I have put this frosting on the Easy Fudge Cake and won the approval of friends. Beats up into a perfect icing. If you do not wish a thick icing, use the rest for fudge. If the icing gets too thick to spread, add a small amount of milk or cream and if making fudge beat until real thick. Enough icing to ice a 9x13 inch cake.

1 c. sugar
2 Tbsp. cocoa
4 Tbsp. butter or margarine
¼ c. milk or cream

Pinch of salt
1 tsp. vanilla
½ c. nuts (optional)

Combine all ingredients, except vanilla. Bring to boil and cook 2 minutes. Add vanilla. Cool and beat. Spread over cake or brownies or put on dish or plate for fudge.

CHOCOLATE CAKE
(Prize winner)

By a friend. Ann Prillaman, who lives at Potomac, II. This recipe was a winner of a 1975 bake-off contest. Makes a large cake, one you'll be proud of.

Mix until smooth then cool:

1 c. unsifted cocoa

2 c. boiling water

Mix at high speed for 5 minutes:

1 c. butter or margarine
2½ c. granulated sugar

4 eggs
1½ tsp. vanilla

Sift together:

2¾ c. flour
2 tsp. baking soda

1 tsp. salt
½ tsp. baking powder

Add dry ingredients alternately with cooled cocoa mixture. Do not overbeat. Divide evenly between 3 layer cake pans. Bake at 350° for 25 to 30 minutes. Cool in pans 10 minutes, remove and cool completely on racks.

Frosting:

1 (6 oz.) pkg. semi-sweet chocolate
½ c. butter or margarine

½ c. cream (Milnot, etc.)
2½ c. confectioners sugar

Heat in a saucepan, then add 2½ cups unsifted confectioners sugar. Mix well.

Note: To add beauty, make small swirls with knife on icing and add nut halves or sprinkle nuts on top (optional).

HICKORY NUT CAKE

I recall as a child, the walnut and hickory nut trees in the pasture. I mashed my thumb many times with the hammer cracking those good nuts. This cake has a lovely, light texture and is full of good nut flavor, that you are sure to enjoy.

½ c. butter
½ c. white shortening
2 c. sugar
1½ c. buttermilk, divided
3 c. sifted cake flour
1 tsp. baking powder

½ tsp. baking soda
½ tsp. salt
1 c. chopped hickory nuts
1 tsp. vanilla
4 egg whites, stiffly beaten

You may substitute pecans or walnuts for hickory nuts. Before assembling cake, sprinkle about 2 teaspoons flour over nuts, tossing to coat; set aside. Cream together the butter, shortening and sugar. Add about ½ cup buttermilk; beat until mixture is fluffy and creamy. Combine the flour, baking powder, soda and salt. Add alternately to creamed mixtue with the remaining buttermilk, beating to blend after each addition. Stir in floured nuts and vanilla. Fold in stiffly beaten egg whites. Spread batter evenly into three greased 9 inch layer pans. Bake at 350° for 25 to 30 minutes or until tested done. Fill layers with vanilla custard or butter icing, and frost top and sides with butter icing.

Note: If you do not like a high three layer cake, assemble a two layer cake and cut the third layer in half to make half a cake. Or, bake cupcakes from remaining batter.

A frown is a smile turned upside down.

PRUNE CAKE

This cake keeps well, if you hide it. Good for the holidays, but delicious anytime.

2 c. flour
Pinch of salt
1 tsp. soda
1 tsp. cinnamon
1 tsp. allspice
1 tsp. nutmeg
1½ c. sugar

Glaze:

1 c. sugar
½ c. buttermilk
½ tsp. vanilla

1 c. cooking oil
1 c. buttermilk
3 eggs
1 tsp. vanilla
1 c. nuts, chopped
1 c. prunes, chopped

1 Tbsp. light corn syrup
1 stick butter

Sift together flour, salt, soda, cinnamon, allspice and nutmeg. Mix in bowl sugar, oil, buttermilk, eggs and vanilla. Mix all together. Fold in nuts and prunes. Grease a tube pan, line with waxed paper and grease paper. Bake 1 hour and 15 minutes at 350°. Cool 15 minutes and remove from pan.

Mix glaze and cook over medium flame, stirring constantly, until it turns caramel color. Pour over cake.

BEST GINGERBREAD

½ c. sugar
1 egg
¼ c. light Brer Rabbit molasses
1 c. flour (don't you dare add more!)
1 tsp. soda

¼ tsp. each cinnamon, ginger,
    nutmeg, salt
½ c. melted butter (you must use
    butter)
½ c. hot water

Mix sugar, egg and molasses. Sift flour, soda and spices; add to sugar mixture. Add hot water to melted butter (¼ cup only), add to the flour mixture. Bake in square pan 8x8 inches greased and floured, about 20 minutes at 350°. When done, while still in pan. pour remaining ¼ cup melted butter over gingerbread, using pastry brush. Serve warm. Whipped cream is optional.

QUICK FUDGE ICING

Many years ago this recipe was given to me from my Aunt Bernice, who lives in Jackson, Ms. I have used this numerous times and shared it many times upon request. Tastes just like fudge and is so easy to make.

1 c. sugar
⅓ c. cocoa
Dash of salt
2 Tbsp. dark Karo Syrup

2 Tbsp. margarine
½ c. milk
1 box powdered sugar

Mix sugar, cocoa and salt together and mix well. Add Karo syrup and milk. Bring to a boil on stove and boil hard for 3 minutes. Remove from stove and add margarine and powdered sugar. Beat until right consistency to spread. If it hardens, simply add a dew drops of milk and beat again.

 The frosting makes a lovely cake
Whether decorated or plain,
But the children's greatest joy is -
To lick the spoon and pan!

GOOEY BUTTER CAKE

1 egg
1 box Duncan Hines butter cake mix
    or yellow cake mix

Topping:

1 box powdered sugar
2 eggs

1 c. chopped nuts

1 stick margarine
1 (8oz.) pkg. cream cheese
    softened

Mix cake ingredients with hands until crumbly. Pat lightly into greased and floured 9x13 inch pan. Mix topping ingredients with electric mixer and pour over cake. Bake at 325° for 35 to 40 minutes.

POPPY SEED CAKE

It is fun to bake cakes. Make someone happy!

1 c. buttermilk
1 c. shortening
3 c. sugar
3 c. flour
6 whole eggs
¼ tsp. soda

½ tsp. salt
1 tsp. vanilla
1 tsp. almond extract
1 tsp. butter flavoring
1 Tbsp. poppy seeds

Glaze:

⅓ c. orange juice
1⅔ c. powdered sugar
1 tsp. vanilla

1 tsp. almond extract
1 tsp. butter flavoring

Soak the poppy seeds in buttermilk overnight. Cream together well, shortening and sugar, and add eggs one at a time. Sift flour, soda, and salt and add to the creamed mixture. Add buttermilk with vanilla, almond extract, and butter flavoring. Bake in a greased and floured Bundt pan in 350° oven for 1 to 1½ hours. Cool 10 minutes, then remove from pan; add the glaze.

Glaze: Bring to a boil and pour over while it is still warm.

HUMMINGBIRD CAKE

"This cake is super moist and super delicious!"

3 c. flour
2 c. sugar
1 tsp. salt
1 tsp. soda
1 tsp. cinnamon
3 eggs

1½ c. salad oil
1½ tsp. vanilla extract
1 (8 oz.) can crushed pineapple
    (undrained)
1 c. chopped pecans or walnuts
2 c. chopped bananas

Combine dry ingredients in a large mixing bowl; add eggs and salad oil, stirring until dry ingredients are moistened. Do not beat. Stir in vanilla, pineapple, pecans and bananas. Spoon batter into 3 well greased and floured 9 inch cake pans. Bake in 350° oven for 25 to 30 minutes or until cake tests done. Cool in pans 10 minutes; remove from pans and cool completely.

Note: Frost with Cream Cheese Frosting (p. 94), sprinkle with chopped pecans or walnuts.

LEMON BUTTER ICING

This is a good icing to frost the soft Sugar Cookies recipes.

¼ stick butter
1 c. confectioners sugar
1 Tbsp. lemon juice

1 Tbsp. milk
1 Tbsp lemon rind

Cream together butter and sugar. Gradually add lemon juice, milk and rind. Beat the icing until it reaches spreading consistency.
Serves 12

POPCORN CAKE
(Delicious)

1 c. sugar
⅓ c. light corn syrup
1 c. whipping cream

1 Tbsp. butter
Popped popcorn

Cook all ingredients until forms a soft ball in cold water. Take off fire and add pinch of soda. Pour over popped corn and stir well. Put in angel food cake pan and put in refrigerator to cool, then serve.

Note: Enough popcorn to fill angel food cake pan is a good measure for amount of popped corn for cake.

CHOCOLATE SHEET CAKE

2 c. sugar
2 c. flour
½ c. buttermilk
1 tsp. soda
2 eggs
½ tsp. salt

1 tsp. vanilla
2 sticks margarine
4 Tbsp. cocoa
1 c. hot water
½ tsp. cinnamon

Frosting:

1 stick margarine
4 Tbsp. cocoa
6 Tbsp. buttermilk

1 lb. box confectioners sugar
1 tsp. vanilla
1 c. nuts, chopped

Cake: Melt margarine; add cocoa and hot water. Bring to a rapid boil. Pour over dry ingredients. Add buttermilk, eggs, and vanilla. Bake in large greased cookie sheet for 15 to 20 minutes at 350°.

Frosting: Melt margarine; add cocoa and buttermilk. Bring to a boil. Boil for 1 minute. Add powdered sugar, vanilla and nuts. Mix thoroughly and place on cake while warm. When cool, cut in bars.

In nothing be anxious, but in everything by prayer and supplication, with Thanksgiving, let your request be made known unto God. Phillipians 4:6

ANGEL FOOD CAKE ICING

An especially good icing for angel food cake that I have used for years, the recipe was given to me from a friend June Duncan, who lives in Potomac, Il., originally her great grandmother's recipe. It makes a lovely glaze that has a delicious flavor.

1 c. sugar   1 c. cream
1 stick butter or margarine

In heavy saucepan, cook ingredients on medium heat stirring occasionally. When starts to thicken stir constantly to keep from scorching. Cook until soft ball can be formed in cold water. Remove from heat and beat with hand mixer until spreading consistency. If thickens add a few drops of cream or milk. Spread on cake.

BLUEBERRY COFFEE CAKE
(Good for a brunch)

2 c. flour   ½ c. milk
1 c. sugar   1 tsp. vanilla
2 tsp. baking powder   1 (18 oz.) blueberry pie filling, or
½ tsp. salt   filling of your choice
½ c. butter   ¼ c. sugar
2 eggs

Combine flour, 1 cup sugar, baking powder and salt. Cut in batter till crumbly. Reserve ½ cup. Beat eggs and milk and vanilla. Add to crumb mixture. Spread in 9x13 inch pan. Combine pie filling and ¼ cup sugar. Spread over batter. Sprinkle with reserve crumbs. Bake in 350° oven for 45 minutes or until done.

Delicious to eat,
Delightful to taste
Gay and attractive
Not a crumb goes to waste!

BANANA CHOCOLATE CAKE
(Oh, so good)

¼ c. soft margarine   2¼ c. cake flour
1 c. sugar   1 tsp. baking powder
2 eggs   1 tsp. baking soda
1 tsp. vanilla   ¾ tsp. salt
1 c. mashed bananas   1 c. chocolate chips
1 c. sour cream   1½ tsp. vanilla

Cream the margarine, sugar and 2 eggs. Add vanilla, mashed bananas. Alternate the sifted dry ingredients with the cup of sour cream. Add chocolate chips. Pour into greased and floured 9x13 inch pan. Bake in 350° oven for 40 to 45 minutes.

Friends are a treasured gift.

TURTLE CAKE

This cake was brought to a reunion by my sister Pat Kelly, who lives at Moberly, Mo. Being simply delicious, it rated high with compliments. If you like chocolate, this cake will rate high with you too!

Mix together:

1 box German chocolate cake mix   **¾ c. melted margarine**
½ c. evaporated milk

Put ½ of the batter into a 9x13 inch pan. Bake for 5 minutes in 350° oven. Cool.

Melt together:

1 (14 oz.) bag caramels   **½ c. evaporated milk**

Pour on top of cake. Sprinkle with large bag semi-sweet chocolate chips and 1 cup chopped pecans. Drop rest of batter over cake by teaspoons. Bake in 350° oven for 20 minutes. Do not overbake.

Note: You may melt caramel in microwave or use double boiler.

"Buy butter, margarine in ¼ pound sticks for easy measuring."

EASY FUDGE CAKE

This cake is rich and moist, easy to make and great for the time you need a small cake.

1 c. cake flour   1 sq. unsweetened chocolate
⅝ c. sugar   ½ c. sour cream
½ tsp. soda   1 egg
½ tsp. salt   3 additional Tbsp. sour cream
1 stick butter or margarine   ½ tsp. vanilla

Melt butter with chocolate; add ½ cup sour cream and vanilla. Pour over sifted dry ingredients. Beat 2 minutes with electric mixer. Add egg and 3 tablespoons sour cream, beat 2 more minutes. Grease and flour 8 inch square or 9 inch round baking dish for batter. Bake 35 minutes in 350° oven. Ice with favorite icing.

It is a good thing
to give thanks unto the
Lord and sing Praises
unto thy Name. Psalms 92:1

PUMPKIN CAKE

2 c. white sugar
4 eggs
1½ c. corn oil
1 tsp. salt
3 tsp. cinnamon
2 tsp. soda

2 tsp. baking powder
2 cups canned pumpkin
1 c. chopped nuts
3 c. flour
½ c. raisins (optional)

Cream together sugar, eggs and corn oil; sift together flour, salt, cinnamon, soda and baking powder and add to creamed mixture alternately with pumpkin; add nuts. Pour into greased cake pan (best in angel food cake pan or Bundt pan) and bake at 350° for 50 to 60 minutes. Glaze with Cream Cheese Frosting (p. 94)

BARB'S STRAWBERRY WHIP CREAM CAKE

A beautiful cake, delicious and served for special occasions, the recipe shared to me from a friend, Barbara Mehlenbacker from Peoria, Il.

1 Duncan Hines yellow cake mix   **Strawberries**
Whipped cream, sweetened

Grease and line with wax paper, or grease and flour, 2 (9 inch) cake pans. Bake cake as directed on package, beating well. Cool and cut layers in two. Carefully put on wax paper, making 4 layers. Assemble together each layer with whipped cream and frozen thawed, drained strawberries, or if strawberries are in season use sweetened fresh strawberries, drained, over the whipped cream on each layer. Arrange whole berries on top of cake to add beauty.

Note: Real whipping cream is best to use.

A recipe that is as old as time itself,
Yet always delightfully new.
They call it simply friendship;
Beloved, tried and true.

Try using a thread instead of a knife when a cake is to be cut in halves.

When the phone rings or something else needs handling when you have messy hands from baking, solve the problem of getting the phone messy by slipping a handy plastic bag over your hand.

PERFECT PIE CRUST

Makes 5 (9 inch) crusts. Very flaky.

4 c. flour
1 Tbsp. sugar
2 tsp. salt
1¾ c. vegetable shortening (Crisco)

½ c. water
1 Tbsp. white or cider vinegar
1 large egg

In large bowl, mix well with fork, the flour, sugar and salt. Add shortening; mix with fork until crumbly. In small bowl, beat water, vinegar and egg. Add to flour mixture and stir until moistened. Wrap each in plastic or waxed paper and chill at least ½ hour. Roll out between lightly floured waxed paper. For baked pie shell place dough in pie pan, prick bottom and sides with fork. Bake in 375° preheated oven for 12 to 15 minutes or until lightly browned. For two crust pies, follow recipe. Dough can be kept up to 3 days refrigerated. Let soften at room temperature before rolling out. Do not use lard, margarine, butter or oil.

MACAROON PIE

My good friend and neighbor, Julie Charles, shared this delicious recipe with me, a specialty of Lindburners Restaurant in Macon, Georgia. You must try this.

16 Saltine crackers,
  crushed
½ pkg. pitted dates
¾ c. chopped nuts

¾ c. sugar
½ t. baking powder
4 egg whites
1 t. almond extract

Beat egg whites, add sugar gradually, Add other ingredients gradually. Pour into "Pam" or buttered pie pan. Bake for 12-15 minutes in 350 degree oven. Cool. Top with whipped cream.

VELVETY CUSTARD PIE

9-inch unbaked pie shell
4 slightly beaten eggs
½ c. sugar
¼ t. salt

1 t. vanilla
2½ c. milk, scalded
½ teaspoon nutmeg

Beat eggs slightly, add sugar, salt and vanilla, and nutmeg. Mix well. Slowly stir in hot milk. Pour at once into the unbaked pie shell. Bake in preheated oven at 450 degrees for 10 minutes. Reduce heat to 350 degrees and bake until knife inserted in pie comes out clean. Approximately 20 minutes.
Sprinkle additional nutmeg across top of pie.

Doug, Tim, Jim, Brad, Greg, & Bill

BLACKBERRY COBBLER

As a young girl, my grandmother took me blackberry picking and I thoroughly enjoyed it. Through the years I have found much pleasure in getting into the blackberry patch. I usually took someone with me or one of my little ones. A bucket in both hands, we would walk down the railroad tracks, climb over a fence and into the pasture we would go. Sometimes we would have to tramp down weeds and vines to get to the berries. I would get so scratched up, but I didn't mind, because that was my idea of a good time, and I knew that Sonny liked the cobblers so well and our little guys liked the jelly made from the berries. What a rewarding joy that was to me. An easy recipe to put together, you'll enjoy too, if you like blackberries!

2 qt. blackberries
2 c. sugar

7 tbsp. flour
Butter or margarine

Roll out pie crust to fit 9x13 inch pan. Mix sugar, and flour together and mix lightly with berries, not crushing berries. Place over pie crust and dot very well with butter or margarine. (Liquid Parkay is great for this.) Place top crust on top of berries, cutting off excess pie crust. Squeeze pie dough edges together. (Brush top of dough with cream or milk, or egg white, optional.) Sprinkle sugar on top of crust. Bake in preheated 350° oven for 1 hour or until crust is medium in color.

Note: Frozen blackberries may be used.

SOUTHERN CHESS PIE

Delicious old southern recipe and easy to make. It is an enriched egg custard type of pie.

3 eggs
1½ c. sugar
½ c. melted margarine
⅓ c. buttermilk

2½ Tbsp. yellow corn meal (white may be used)
1 tsp. pure vanilla or butternut-vanilla flavoring

Mix together and pour in unbaked pie shell. Bake at 350° for 40 minutes. Add coconut sprinkled on top, or pecans if desired.

To prevent soggy pie crust in an unbaked pie shell, brush with a thin coating of egg white. Especially good for fruit pies.

Cut drinking straws into short lengths and insert through slits in pie crusts to prevent juice from running over in the oven and permit steam to escape.

Put cream, milk or brush egg white on top of two crust pies for a nice brown pie.

Set pies and cobblers on a rack to cool and the bottom crust will not be soggy.

I can do all things through Christ, who strengthens me. Philippians 4:13

PINEAPPLE PIE

1 c. sugar
¼ tsp. salt
3 Tbsp. cornstarch
1 egg

1 can crushed pineapple with juice
1 Tbsp. butter

Cook over medium heat until thickens. Boil 1 minute. Add 1 tablespoon margarine. Pour into 8 inch unbaked pie crust. Bake in 425° oven for 25 to 30 minutes.

LEMON MERINGUE PIE

A friend, Pam Ashcraft, serves this superb lemon pie at her "Ye Cozy Tea Shoppe" in Monticello, Il. The most impressive tea shoppe of its kind, the atmosphere is tremendous, every item on the menu made from scratch. Pam is indeed a gourmet cook.

1½ c. sugar	5 egg yolks, beaten
1½ c. water	½ c. lemon juice
½ tsp. salt	3 Tbsp. butter
½ c. cornstarch	1 tsp. lemon peel (optional)
⅓ c. water	

Bring to a boil the 1½ cups sugar, 1½ cups water and salt. In small bowl, mix ⅓ cup water with ½ cup cornstarch. Pour into boiling sugar and water mixture, and cook on high until thick and clear. Remove from heat. In bowl mix egg yolks, lemon juice, lemon peel and butter. Pour into clear mixture and stir well. Cook 2 minutes longer, stirring well. Allow filling to cool before filling pie shell. Dust the pie shell with powdered sugar.

Meringue for Lemon Meringue Pie:

6 egg whites	¼ tsp. salt
½ c. sugar	1 pinch of cream of tartar

Place all ingredients in mixing bowl and mix with electric mixer for several minutes, until mixture forms very stiff peaks that are shiny. Spread on pie and seal edges well. Design meringue with spoon. Place pie on rack on the second position from the top of the oven. Bake at 375° until meringue is nicely browned. When cooled, cut through pie with wet knife.

There are only two lasting things we can give our children.
One is roots; the other wings.

FRESH STRAWBERRY PIE

You'll be proud to serve this pie to your guests.

1½ c. sugar
¼ c. cornstarch
Dash of salt
1½ c. water

2 drops of red food coloring
1 box strawberry Jello gelatin
Whipping cream
1 qt. fresh strawberries

Mix the sugar, cornstarch and salt together in saucepan, gradually add water. Cook until thick and clear. Add red food coloring and strawberry Jello; cool. Add 1 quart fresh strawberries. Pour in a baked pie shell and refrigerate. Before serving, add whipped cream and garnish with a fresh strawberry.

Note: I like to put swirls of whipped cream on the pie with a decorating bag using a medium size star tube. Makes the pie very attractive.

Pie Crust for Strawberry Pie:

A friend, Jeanette Knight shared this good crust recipe with me.

1½ c. flour
1 tsp. salt
1 tsp. sugar

2 Tbsp. cold milk
½ c. oil

Mix with fork and press in pan. Bake in 400° oven for 10 to 12 minutes until lightly browned.

FRESH PEACH PIE

The touch of cinnamon enhances this pie. Serve with a dip of ice cream for extra goodness!

1 c. sugar
4 Tbsp. flour
½ tsp. cinnamon

5½ c. sliced peaches
1½ tsp. lemon juice
2 Tbsp. melted margarine

Mix sugar, flour, margarine, spices; mix peaches with lemon juice. Add flour mixture; mix carefully. Turn into a pastry lined pan. Cover with top crust. Bake in a 400° oven until crust is golden brown.

Do what you can, with what you have, where you are.

CHIFFON PUMPKIN PIE

A different pumpkin pie, well worth the little extra effort.

1 env. Knox sparkling gelatine
¼ c. cold water
1¼ c. pumpkin
½ c. milk
1 c. sugar

3 eggs
½ tsp. ginger
½ tsp. cinnamon
½ tsp. nutmeg
½ tsp. salt

To slightly beaten egg yolks, add ½ cup of the sugar, pumpkin, spices and salt. Mix and add milk. Cook until pretty thick on medium heat. Soften gelatine in the ¼ cup water. Put immediately in pumpkin mixture and let cool. Beat 3 egg whites until stiff. Slowly add rest of the sugar. Gently fold into the pumpkin mixture. Let cool in refrigerator.

APPLE SLICES
(Delicious)

2 c. flour
⅔ c. shortening
½ tsp. salt
1 egg yolk
½ c. milk
10 apples, peeled and sliced

1½ c. sugar
2 Tbsp. flour
3 Tbsp. margarine or butter
Cinnamon
1 egg white

Mix and crumble into bowl the flour, shortening and salt. Beat egg yolk of one egg and ½ cup milk, and stir into flour mixture, using a fork. Divide dough in halves. Press half in bottom of pan, or roll out on floured waxed paper, cold and put in bottom. Cover with apples. Mix 1½ cups sugar with 2 tablespoons flour. Sprinkle over apples. Sprinkle cinnamon lightly over top. Dot with 3 tablespoons margarine or butter. Add top crust. Beat egg white and brush over top. Bake in 375° oven for 45 minutes. Cool slightly and dribble powdered sugar icing on top.

KINDNESS

A little word in kindness spoken,
  A motion, or a tear,
Has often healed the heart that's broken
  And made a friend sincere.

A word, a look, has crushed to earth
  Full many a budding flower,
Which, had a smile but owned its birth,
  Would bless life's darkest hour.

Then deem it not an idle thing
  A pleasant word to speak;
The face you wear, the thought you bring,
  A heart may heal or break.

APPLE ROLL

A delicious recipe, from my niece Mary McKeown, who is a homemaker in Moberly, Mo., and enjoys the challenge of new recipes and entertaining guests.

Sauce:

2 c. sugar
2 Tbsp. flour
2 Tbsp. butter

½ tsp. salt
2 c. hot water
½ lemon, sliced

Mix in saucepan and let come to a boil. Set aside.

2 c. sifted flour
2 tsp. baking powder
1 tsp. salt

1 Tbsp. lard or Crisco
1 Tbsp. butter
⅞ c. milk

Mix and roll in lengthwise strips, cover with chopped apples, cinnamon and brown sugar. Roll, slice about 1½ inches. Place in pan and pour sauce around the rolls. Bake in 350° oven until apples are done.

CHERRY SLICES

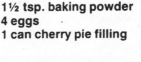

These bars are a year around favorite.

1 c. margarine
1¾ c. sugar
2½ c. flour
1 tsp. vanilla

1½ tsp. baking powder
4 eggs
1 can cherry pie filling

Combine margarine, sugar, flour, vanilla, baking powder and eggs. Beat until fluffy. Dough will be thick. Spread half of dough on greased jelly roll pan. Spread cherry pie filling over dough. Top with rest of dough. Bake in 350° oven for 40 minutes. Cut into bars when cool.

APPLE DUMPLINGS

Have fun today! Make these scrumptious apple dumplings. Always a favorite, serve with a scoop of ice cream.

1. Regular pie crust recipe. Roll out dough. Cut in 5 inch squares.
2. Place 1 and ½ chopped medium apple on each square. Sprinkle 3 teaspoons sugar, a splash of cinnamon and pats of butter on each dumpling. Fold up all 4 edges and gently squeeze together and place in baking pans.
3. Bring to boil 2 cups sugar, 2 cups water and ⅓ cup butter. Pour syrup around dumplings and bake in preheated 350° oven for 40 minutes or until dough is light brown.

Note: I sometimes use my regular pie crust recipe. Also ½ apple on each circle can be used, using 1 teaspoon sugar, dash of cinnamon and small pat of butter on each circle, folding dough over.

No one can give you better advice than yourself.

COCONUT PIE

When I made pies for the restaurant, rated at the top of "Peoples Choice" was coconut. Real homemade pies became extremely popular. I received much satisfaction from pleasing our customers. I'd like to share this recipe with you.

1 c. sugar	4 egg yolks
8 Tbsp. cornstarch	2 Tbsp. butter
⅛ tsp. salt	1½ tsp. vanilla extract
3 c. milk	¾ c. coconut

To make this pie, a wooden spoon with a square end is great for stirring. Combine sugar, cornstarch and salt in heavy saucepan. Mix well. Add ½ cup of the milk and mix well. Add remaining milk. Stir constantly on medium heat until thickens. Remove from heat and pour at about ½ cup of the pudding into the egg yolks and mix, as this keeps the egg yolk smooth. Return to pan and add the butter, vanilla and coconut, stirring constantly on medium heat 2 additional minutes. Pour into baked pie shell.

Top with meringue while filling is still hot or refrigerate if you wish a whipped cream topping with toasted coconut. When using whipped cream, after putting the whipped cream on the top, I enjoyed using my cake decorator to make this pie really attractive, adding whipped cream to decorating bag, using the medium star tip around the edge. Even after the pie is cut and ready to serve you can decorate the sides too!

Note: To toast coconut, put coconut in shallow pan in 350° oven until lightly browned. Watch closely, to prevent scorching. To make chocolate pie, simply add 2 tablespoons cocoa to dry ingredients and follow same instructions. To make peanut butter pie, add 2 tablespoons of peanut butter or more to your liking and ¼ teaspoon black walnut flavoring.

I will always carry a "bag of smiles,"
And hope to spread happiness for miles and miles.

PECAN PIE

3 eggs, slightly beaten	¼ c. melted butter or margarine
¾ c. sugar	1 Tbsp. lemon juice (optional)
1 c. white Karo syrup	1 tsp. vanilla flavoring
1 or ½ c. chopped pecans	

Combine ingredients and pour into unbaked pie shell. Bake for 10 minutes in 450° oven, then turn to 300° and bake for 45 minutes to 1 hour.

Note: A secret to a good pecan pie is to not use mixer, only for beating the eggs slightly, then stir ingredients together.

MERINGUE

4 egg whites	8 Tbsp. sugar

Beat egg whites for 1 minute or until frothy. Add sugar and beat until meringue is very stiff, but not dry., Spread on pie. Bake until light brown.

DIFFERENT PECAN PIE

1 pkg. vanilla pudding
1 c. white corn syrup
¾ c. evaporated milk

1 egg, slightly beaten
1 c. chopped pecans
1 unbaked pie shell

Blend the pudding and syrup together. Gradually add the milk and egg. Stir in the pecans. Pour this mixture into the pie shell, and bake at 375° for about 40 minutes, until the top is firm and begins to crack. Cool at least 3 hours before serving.

JAPANESE FRUIT PIE

2 c. sugar
4 eggs
¾ c. melted margarine
1 c. raisins
1 c. nuts

1 c. coconut
1 tsp. vanilla
1 Tbsp. vinegar
½ tsp. burnt sugar flavoring
(optional)

Mix sugar, eggs and margarine, and then all remaining ingredients; pour evenly into unbaked pie shell. Bake in 350° oven for 35 to 40 minutes, until set. Remove from oven. Serve warm or cold.

AUNT AGNES'S ONE CRUST APPLE PIE

If apple pie is one of your favorites, then you'll enjoy this. Easy to make, sure to please.

¾ c. sugar
1 Tbsp. flour
1 stick butter
1 tsp. vanilla

1 tsp. cinnamon
2 eggs
1½ c. tart shredded apples

Cream all together except apples. Stir in apples. Pour into unbaked crust. Bake at 350° for 50 minutes.

Apple pie without cheese is like a hug without a squeeze.

111

PAT'S CHOCOLATE DREAM PIE

Very impressive, easy to make and delicious!! After sampling at a church pot luck, I decided I needed the recipe and was surprised when I found it was made with instant pudding. For a quick dessert, you'll enjoy it too!!

1 pkg. graham crackers   **¼ c. sugar**
1 stick butter or margarine

Crush graham crackers with rolling pin. Add sugar, stir in melted butter. Press into pie shell. Bake 8 minutes in 350° oven. Cool.

2 pkg. (4 serving size) instant   **4 c. cold milk**
chocolate pudding

Mix pudding and milk together until whipped good. Pour over graham cracker crust. Spread top with whipped topping and refrigerate. (A whipped topping, such as Dream Whip, that you add milk to and whip is the best topping for this pie.)

CHERRY PIE

2 c. sugar   **1 Tbsp. butter**
5 Tbsp. cornstarch   **¼ tsp. almond extract**
½ c. cherry juice   **4 c. cherries (unsweetened)**
½ tsp. salt

Mix sugar, salt, cornstarch and juice in saucepan. Cook until begins to boil rapidly, stirring constantly. Add drained cherries and continue gently until desired thickness is reached. Remove from heat and add butter. Cool. Pour into pastry lined pan. Add top crust or strips of pastry. Bake at 450° for 10 minutes, then reduce the temperature to 375° for 20 minutes.

RITZ CRACKER PIE
(Tastes like pecan pie)

3 egg whites, beaten stiff   **½ tsp. baking powder**
1 c. sugar

Beat again until stiff.

Add:

25 to 30 Ritz crackers   **½ tsp. vanilla**
1 c. chopped nuts

Butter 9 inch pie plate and pour in. Bake in 350° oven for 25 to 30 minutes or until golden brown. Cool and cover with whipped cream.

OATMEAL PIE

3 eggs, slightly beaten
1 c. waffle syrup
½ c. coconut
1 c. oatmeal

1 tsp. vanilla
½ stick margarine
½ c. evaporated milk

Mix ingredients together. Bake in a slow oven until solid and brown.

MOTHER'S PIE CRUST
(A great flaky crust)

3 c. flour
1 c. plus 2 Tbsp. butter Crisco or
    lard
1 tsp. salt

1 egg
7 Tbsp. water
1 Tbsp. vinegar

Blend well the flour, salt and Crisco with pastry blender or fork. In small bowl, add water, egg and vinegar and mix well. Stir into first mixture and form into pie crust. Do not overhandle. Roll out between floured wax paper. (If baking pie shell alone, fit dough into pie plate, then prick dough thoroughly with fork over the entire surface.) Bake at 375° for 10 minutes or until very light brown. Will make 4 crusts.

Love Beareth All Things

LOVE

Love is patient, love is kind. It does not
envy, it does not boast, it is not proud. It is not rude,
It is not self-seeking, it is not easily angered, it keeps no record of wrongs. Love does not delight in evil but rejoices with truth.
It always trusts, always hopes, always perserves. Love never fails.

I Cor. 13:4-8

BETSY ROSS CAKE

Add some excitement to the 4th of July by creating a cake to resemble our first American flag. Not only beautiful, but delicious too!

1 c. butter, softened	Grated rind and juice of 1
5 eggs, separated	lemon
½ tsp. baking soda	1 c. milk
4 c. sifted cake flour	1 tsp. vanilla
3 c. sugar	

Cream butter and sugar until light and fluffy. Add egg yolks, grated rind and juice of lemon, baking soda, vanilla, flour and milk. Mix until well blended. Beat egg whites stiff but not dry. Fold into batter. Pour into greased 13×9 inch baking pan. Bake in 325° oven for about 45 minutes or until done. Cool cake and frost with the White Chocolate Cream Cheese Frosting.

White Chocolate Cream Cheese Frosting:

4 c. confectioners sugar	1 (8 oz.) pkg. cream cheese
6 oz. white chocolate	2 tsp. vanilla
3 Tbsp. butter	

Gradually beat sugar into cream cheese until evenly blended. Melt chocolate. Add to butter and cool. Blend with cream cheese mixture. Add vanilla and mix well. Reserve ¼ of the frosting if decorating.

Arrange drained blueberries in a 4x6 rectangle in upper left hand corner. With the point of a knife, trace wavy 2 inch stripes from left to right across cake. Set strawberries, pointed end up, in alternate stripes. Pipe remaining frosting in remaining stripes and pipe a few stars on the blueberry field to resemble our first American flag. Great for a party cake!

Cookies
and
Candy

TEMPERATURE TESTS
FOR CANDY MAKING

There are two different methods of determining when candy has been cooked to the proper consistency. One is by using a candy thermometer in order to record degrees, the other is by using the cold water test. The chart below will prove useful in helping to follow candy recipes:

TYPE OF CANDY	DEGREES	COLD WATER
Fondant, Fudge	234 - 238°	Soft Ball
Divinity, Caramels	245 - 248°	Firm Ball
Taffy	265 - 270°	Hard Ball
Butterscotch	275 - 280°	Light Crack
Peanut Brittle	285 - 290°	Hard Crack
Caramelized Sugar	310 - 321°	Caramelized

In using the cold water test, use a fresh cupful of cold water for each test. When testing, remove the candy from the fire and pour about ½ teaspoon of candy into the cold water. Pick the candy up in the fingers and roll into a ball if possible.

In the SOFT BALL TEST the candy will roll into a soft ball which quickly loses its shape when removed from the water.

In the FIRM BALL TEST the candy will roll into a firm but not hard ball. It will flatten out a few minutes after being removed from water.

In the HARD BALL TEST the candy will roll into a hard ball which has lost almost all plasticity and will roll around on a plate on removal from the water.

In the LIGHT CRACK TEST the candy will form brittle threads which will soften on removal from the water.

In the HARD CRACK TEST the candy will form brittle threads in the water which will remain brittle after being removed from the water.

In CARAMELIZING, the sugar first melts then becomes a golden brown. It will form a hard brittle ball in cold water.

COOKIES AND CANDY

THE OLD PANTRY

It stood next to the kitchen,
only a door between;
It held the many goodies
about which children dream.

Sweet jellies, red and purple,
(wild strawberry and grape);
Fresh pies and homemade cookies
and tasty chocolate cake.

It stood next to the kitchen,
with just a door between ...
The old pantry at Grandma's
where goodies reigned supreme.

ALMOND COOKIES

A favorite cookie recipe of my friend, Dorothy Palmer from Chicago, Il. It has been my pleasure to enjoy fun, food and fellowship with friends like Dorothy.

1 c. soft butter	**¼ tsp. salt**
⅓ c. sugar	**⅔ c. blanched almonds, ground, or**
1⅔ c. flour	**chopped very fine**

Mix butter and sugar thoroughly. Sift the flour and salt together and stir into the first mixture. Stir in almonds. Chill dough thoroughly. Pinch pieces size of walnut. Roll between fingers until round ball stage. Place on ungreased cookie sheet. Press ½ almond on top of each cookie. At same time, flattening slightly. Bake in 325° oven for about 15 minutes or until beginning to brown slightly around edges.

ROOT BEER COOKIES

1 c. brown sugar, packed	**1 tsp. root beer extract**
½ c. butter or margarine	**1¾ c. all-purpose flour**
1 egg	**½ tsp. baking soda**
¼ c. buttermilk	**½ tsp. salt**

Mix the first 5 ingredients well to a smooth batter. Add dry ingredients and mix well. Put 1 teaspoon dough 2 inches apart on greased cookie sheet. Bake in 350° oven for 6 to 8 minutes.

Root Beer Glaze:

2 c. powdered sugar	**1½ tsp. root beer extract**
⅓ c. butter or margarine	**2 Tbsp. hot water**

Stir and mix well. Brush on top of hot cookies. Will produce approximately 42 cookies.

A sense of humor is like a needle and thread. It will patch up so many things.

DATE AND NUT COOKIES

A very good recipe of our Great Grandmother Parsons.

2 eggs
½ c. margarine
1 c. sugar
¾ tsp. cinnamon
¾ tsp. soda

1 ¾ c. flour
½ tsp. salt
3 Tbsp. hot water
1 c. dates, chopped
1 c. nuts, chopped

Cream eggs, margarine and sugar. Add sifted dry ingredients and hot water. Add in dates and nuts and mix well. Bake in 350° oven for 10 minutes or light brown in color.

BAKING THE CHRISTMAS COOKIES

Mother is making the dough for the cookies,
Ready to please her four little rookies
Out from the oven, all spicy and hot,
Now for the icing ... ready or not!
Red for the ornaments - green for the trees,
Frosting the cookies is really a breeze.
Sister has chosen the bells and the chickens,
The boys have decided on frosting bowl lickin's!
Now the children have left - their work is all done,
But Mother's still busy - her job's just begun;
She cleans up the sugar that's spilled on the floor,
She washes the bowls and silver galore.
Into the jars she packs cookies, airtight,
And hopes - come Christmas - there'll still be a bite!

SANTA'S WHISKERS

1 c. margarine or butter
1 c. sugar
2 Tbsp. milk
1 tsp. vanilla
2½ c. flour

1 c. finely chopped red or green
    candied cherries
½ c. finely chopped pecans
1 c. flaked coconut

Beat butter, sugar until fluffy. Add milk and vanilla; stir in flour, then cherries and pecans. Shape into three, seven inch rolls. Roll dough in coconut to coat outside. Wrap in waxed paper or clear plastic wrap. Chill thoroughly. Cut into ¼ inch slices. Place on ungreased cookie sheet. Bake in 375° oven for 11 minutes or until edges are golden. Makes approximately 80 cookies.

Like the honey to the bee,
So are cookies to the tea.

THE WORLD'S BEST COOKIES

These cookies stay moist, keep beautifully and the perfect gift. The recipe makes a huge batch. For extra sweetness, sprinkle warm cookies with sugar.

1 c. butter or margarine
1 c. brown sugar, packed
1 egg
1 c. salad oil
1 c. rolled oats
½ c. Angel Flake coconut
½ c. chopped pecans or English
   walnuts

3½ c. sifted flour
1 tsp. soda
1 tsp. salt
1 tsp. vanilla
1 c. crushed corn flakes

Cream together butter and sugars until light and fluffy. Add egg and vanilla, mixing well. Add salad oil, mixing well. Add oats, cornflakes, coconut and nuts, stir well. Add flour, soda and salt. Mix well, then form into balls the size of small walnuts. Place on ungreased cookie sheet. Flatten with fork dipped in water. Bake in 350 ° oven for 12 minutes. Allow to cool on cookie sheet for few minutes before removing from pan.

A good laugh is sunshine in the house.

CHOCOLATE SOFT COOKIES

Mix:

½ c. margarine or butter
1 c. sugar

1 egg

Add:

¾ c. sour buttermilk
1 tsp. vanilla
1¾ c. flour

½ tsp. salt
½ c. cocoa
1 c. nuts, broken

Chill 1 hour. Drop by teaspoonful on greased cookie sheet at 400° for 7 to 8 minutes.

 ## RICE KRISPIE KRITTERS

¼ c. butter
1 teaspoon vanilla

2½ dozen marshmellows
5 cups rice krispies

Melt butter and marshmellows in top of double boiler, over hot warm water until syrupy. Add vanilla, Pour over Krispies, in a large bowl, stir briskly. Press in buttered pan. When cool, cut in squares. Ready to eat!

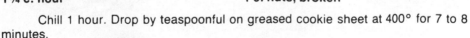

CHOCOLATE CHIP COOKIES

1 c. margarine
¾ c. brown sugar
¼ c. white sugar
2 eggs
1 pkg. instant vanilla pudding

2¼ c. flour
1 tsp. baking soda
1 (12 oz.) pkg. chocolate chips
1 tsp. vanilla

Mix well the first 5 ingredients. Add rest of ingredients. Bake in 350° oven for 8 to 10 minutes.

FINNISH PECAN BALLS

A cookie that melts in your mouth, so simple to make.

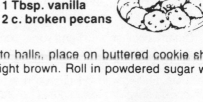

½ lb. butter
4 Tbsp. sugar
2 c. flour

1 Tbsp. vanilla
2 c. broken pecans

Blend ingredients thoroughly, roll into balls, place on buttered cookie sheet. Bake in 350° oven for 20 minutes or very light brown. Roll in powdered sugar while warm.

GREAT OATMEAL BARS

2 sticks margarine, softened
1 c. brown sugar
1 c. white sugar
2 eggs
1 tsp. vanilla

1½ c. flour
1 tsp. soda
3 c. oatmeal
1 tsp. salt

Cream margarine, sugars, eggs and vanilla. Sift dry ingredients and add to the creamed mixture, mixing well. Spread in a sheet cake pan, 11x14 inches. Bake at 350° for 30 minutes or until toothpick is clean.

Note: Three-fourths cup raisins optional.

HELLO DOLLY BARS

Make someone happy today! Bake these cookies and share with a friend. So easy and delicious!

2 c. graham cracker crumbs
1 stick butter
1 c. coconut

1 (6 oz.) milk chocolate chips
1 (6 oz.) butterscotch chips
1 can Eagle Brand milk

Place graham crackers and melted butter in bottom of 9x13 inch dish, then sprinkle coconut, milk chocolate chips and butterscotch chips on top and pour Eagle Brand milk over this. Bake in 350° oven until chips have melted; cool and cut into squares.

LEMON LOVE NOTES

½ c. butter
1 c. flour, sifted
¼ c. powdered sugar
1 c. sugar
2 Tbsp. flour

½ tsp. baking powder
2 eggs, beaten
2 Tbsp. lemon juice
2 tsp. grated lemon rind

Combine the first 3 ingredients; mix well and press into an ungreased 8 inch square pan. Bake at 350° for 8 minutes. Cool in pan. Combine sugar, flour, and baking powder. Add eggs, lemon juice and rind. Mix well. Pour over crust. Bake at 350° for 25 minutes. Cool. Sprinkle with powdered sugar, cut into squares. Makes 16.

HOLIDAY FRUIT COOKIES

1 c. butter
2 c. brown sugar
2 eggs
1 Tbsp. vanilla
½ c. buttermilk
3½ c. flour

1 tsp. soda
1 tsp. salt
1½ c. pecans, chopped
2 c. candied cherries
2 c. dates, chopped

Cream well the butter, brown sugar, eggs and vanilla. Add the buttermilk. Sift together the flour, soda and salt. Add the cherries, nuts and chopped dates. Chill for 4 hours. Drop by teaspoons on a greased cookie sheet. Bake for 8 to 10 minutes.

PAT'S PEANUT BUTTER COOKIES
(Soft and delicious!)

1 c. margarine
1 c. brown sugar
1 c. white sugar
2 eggs
1 small pkg. vanilla instant pudding

1 c. peanut butter
1 tsp. vanilla
2½ c. unsifted flour
2 tsp. baking soda
Pinch of salt

Mix first 5 ingredients together and add peanut butter and vanilla. Mix flour, soda and salt. Add to other mixture. Make into small balls and place on lightly greased cookie sheet. Make crisscrosses with fork. Bake in 350° oven for 10 minutes.

Variation: For an excellent Cinnamon Sugar Cookie use same ingredients, omitting peanut butter and adding 2 teaspoons cinnamon. Make balls size of walnut and dip into sugar and cinnamon mixture. (One-fourth cup sugar and ¼ teaspoon cinnamon.)

A day without orange juice is like a day without sunshine.

PECAN KISSES

½ c. egg whites (measure), beaten into peaks
1½ c. sugar (add to egg whites gradually)

¼ tsp. salt
½ tsp. vanilla
2½ c. chopped pecans

Drop on ungreased cookie sheet about 2 inches apart (one teaspoon for each cookie). Bake at 325° for 20 minutes or until a light tan. Remove from oven and place pan on wet towel for a few minutes. Remove cookies with pancake turner.

SNICKERDOODLES

A very good cookie, semi-soft. Do not overbake.

Mix:

1 c. shortening
1½ c. sugar

2 eggs
1 tsp. vanilla

Then add:

2¾ c. flour
2 tsp. cream of tartar

1 tsp. soda
½ tsp. salt

Chill dough few minutes. Roll into walnut size balls. Roll in mixture of 2 table-spoons sugar and 2 teaspoons cinnamon. Place on ungreased cookie sheet. Bake 9 minutes at 400°

Homemade cookies, nice and neat,
What could be a better treat?

DONNA'S JELLY COOKIES

½ c. shortening
2 tsp. baking powder
2 c. flour
1 egg
1 tsp. vanilla

4 Tbsp. cold water
1 c. brown sugar
¼ tsp. salt
1 tsp. soda
Jelly

Combine sugar, shortening and egg. Sift together dry ingredients. Add to creamy mixture. Add water and mix well. Drop by spoonfuls on greased cookie sheet. Make thumb impression and fill with favorite jelly. Bake in 350° oven for 10 minutes.

ALMOND BARK SURPRISE COOKIE

A quick treat. The surprise is that you cannot tell they were made with Ritz Crackers.

Simply melt chocolate almond bark. Spread peanut butter between Ritz Crackers. Coat each side with melted almond bark.

RICE KRISPIE BALLS

My favorite of the unbaked cookie. Easy to make and great for the holidays.

1 stick margarine
1 c. sugar
1 c. chopped dates
1 slightly beaten egg

3 c. Rice Krispies
½ c. chopped pecans or English walnuts

Melt margarine in pan. Add sugar and chopped dates. Add slightly beaten egg. Stir and cook over low heat until thick, about 5 minutes. Remove from heat, add Rice Krispies and nuts. Pour out on waxed paper and let mixture cool enough to make into balls. Roll in powdered sugar.

BUGS BUNNY BARS
(Children think these are great!)

4 eggs, beaten
2 c. sugar
1½ c. liquid oil
2 c. flour
1 tsp. vanilla
2 tsp. soda

1 tsp. salt
1 tsp. cinnamon
1 c. nuts
3 small jars strained baby food carrots

Combine eggs, sugar and oil. Add vanilla and flour, soda, salt and cinnamon. Stir in nuts and baby food carrots. Spread on cookie sheet and bake in 350° oven for 20 to 25 minutes. When cool, frost with Cream Cheese Frosting (p. 94).

DELICIOUS COOKIES

½ c. margarine
1 c. salad oil
1 c. brown sugar
1 c. white sugar
1 egg
2 tsp. vanilla
1 tsp. coconut flavoring
3½ c. sifted flour

1 tsp. salt
1 tsp. soda
1 tsp. cream of tartar
1 c. rolled oats
1 c. coconut
1 c. Rice Krispies
1 (6 oz.) bag chocolate chips

Blend margarine and oil. Add sugars, egg and flavorings. Beat well with mixer. Sift dry ingredients; mix into cream mixture. Stir in oats, coconut, Rice Krispies, chocolate chips. Drop onto greased cookie sheet. Bake till lightly browned for 12 minutes at 350°. (May want to flatten with fork.)

KINDNESS

*I shall pass through this world but once.
If, therefore, there be any kindess
I can show,
or any good thing I can do,
let me do it now;
let me not defer it or neglect it,
for I shall not pass this way again.*

—*Grellet*

BUTTER PECAN TURTLE COOKIES

Crust:

2 c. all-purpose flour
1 c. firmly packed brown sugar

½ c. butter

Caramel layer:

⅔ c. butter
½ c. packed brown sugar
1 c. whole pecan halves (not
    chopped)

1 c. milk chocolate chips

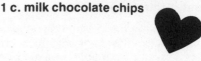

Preheat oven to 350°. Combine crust ingredients, mix at medium speed, scraping sides of bowl often, 2 to 3 minutes or until well mixed and particles are fine. Pat firmly into ungreased 9x13 inch pan. Sprinkle pecans evenly over unbaked crust. Prepare caramel layer; pour evenly over pecans and crust. Bake near center of 350° oven for 20 minutes or until entire caramel layer is bubbly and crust is light golden brown. Remove from oven. Immediately sprinkle with chips. Allow chips to melt slightly (2 or 3 minutes). Slightly swirl chips as they melt; leave some whole for a marbled effect. Cool completely; cut into squares. Yields 3 dozen.

OATMEAL COOKIES

2 sticks margarine or butter
1 c. white sugar
1 c. brown sugar
2 eggs
2 tsp. vanilla
1½ c. flour

1 tsp. salt
1 tsp. soda
3 c. instant oatmeal
1 c. each dates, chopped, nuts,
    chopped and coconut

Cream sugars with margarine. Add vanilla and eggs; mix in flour, salt and soda that have been sifted together. Last, add oatmeal, dates, coconut, and nuts.

Note: Raisins can be used instead of dates and coconut is optional.

BANANA BARS

1½ c. sugar
2 eggs
½ c. butter or 1 stick margarine
3 bananas
1 tsp. baking powder
1 tsp. salt

1 tsp. baking soda
2 c. flour
1½ tsp. cinnamon
½ c. milk
½ c. chopped nuts (optional)

Cream sugar, oleo and eggs; add bananas and milk; add other ingredients. Bake at 350° for 25 to 30 minutes. Cut into squares.

APPLE CRISP
A good quick dessert.

1 c. sifted flour
1 t. baking powder
1 egg beaten
⅓ c. butter

½ t. cinnamon
1½ c. sugar
¾ t. salt
7 apples

Mix apples in ¼ c. sugar and ½ t. cinnamon in a buttered dish. Mix flour, sugar, baking powder, salt and egg together until crumbly and sprinkle over apples. Melt butter, let cool, pour over apples. Bake 30 to 40 minutes in 350 degree oven. Serve with ice cream or whip cream.

ROLLED MOLASSES COOKIES

I have enjoyed making gingerbread men with this recipe.

Mix together thoroughly:

⅔ c. shortening	2 eggs
⅔ c. brown sugar	1⅓ c. molasses

Sift together and stir in:

5½ c. sifted flour	4 tsp. cinnamon
2 tsp. soda	1 tsp. ginger
2 tsp. salt	

Chill dough well. Roll out on floured surface, cut into desired shape. Place 1 inch apart on highly greased sheets. Bake at 350° for 10 to 12 minutes.

Note: For honey dough follow above recipe and substitute honey for molasses, granulated sugar for brown sugar and 1 teaspoon of vanilla in place of cinnamon and ginger.

SOFT SUGAR COOKIES

This is a great roll out cookie! Will keep well in tightly sealed container. Very easy to make.

1 c. butter or margarine	1 c. sour cream
1 c. sugar	1 tsp. vanilla flavoring
3 c. flour	1 tsp. lemon flavoring or lemon
½ tsp. salt	juice
½ tsp. soda	1½ tsp. lemon peel (optional)
2 eggs	

Sift dry ingredients into mixing bowl. Add eggs, sour cream and flavorings. Mix well. Chill cookie dough in refrigerator for 2 hours or overnight covered. The dough must be very cold. Roll out on floured surface and cut with favorite cookie cutters. Use metal spatula to pick up cookie after being cut. Place on ungreased cookie sheets. Bake in 350° oven for 9 minutes or starting to barely brown on the outside of cookie. Do not overbake!

Confectioners' Icing: Melt 4 tablespoons margarine or butter in ¼ cup of milk. Gradually add 2 cups confectioners sugar. Stir in 1 teaspoon vanilla and 3 teaspoons lemon juice or more to taste. The icing needs to be of a medium consistency to spread over cookie. (If too thick, add more milk.) If using colored sugars sprinkle on immediately after cookie is iced.

"A secret for good cookies is not to overbake!"

MAPLE COOKIES

Excellent to keep in freezer for quick cookies. Other flavors may be used instead of maple extract.

4 c. flour
1 tsp. soda
½ tsp. salt
1½ c. shortening
½ c. margarine

1 c. white sugar
1 c. brown sugar
2 eggs
1 tsp. vanilla
2 tsp. maple extract

Mix all ingredients together. Divide dough into 4 parts. Make into logs and put in plastic bags or roll in wax paper. Freeze. Cut in slices and bake at 375° for 10 minutes.

Do you wait for special days
Before you give a gift,
Or do you choose some unmarked time
To give a happy lift?

Gifts need not bear a price tag,
A kind word or a deed,
These are the daily gifts,
Folks want, and badly need.

The value of a gift depends
On how it's wrapped and tied.
If the cords are made of gladness
And there's love inside.

CARAMELS

1 c. white sugar
1 c. light corn syrup
⅛ tsp. salt
2 Tbsp. butter

1 c. cream
1 tsp. vanilla
1 additional c. cream

Boil ingredients to soft ball stage. Slowly add 1 cup additional cream and cook till forms a firm ball dropped in cold water. Pour in greased pan and do not beat. Set until cool. Cut in squares and wrap.

I have used this recipe for Pecan Logs, using the Divinity recipe for the inside. Makes a large amount.

Note: Cooking to very firm ball stage is important.

QUICK CARAMEL APPLES

A real treat that is easy, quick and delious.

Melt a lb. bag of carmels in the mircowave or a double boiler. Add 6 or 7 tablespoons of cream or evaporated milk. stir well. Dribble over apples that have been cut in wedges. A apple slicer works great.

Note: You might want to use just a few caramels. If so, just add less cream to consistency desired for caramel apples.

CHOCOLATE TURTLES

1 lb. caramels
2 Tbsp. water
½ lb. salted nuts

1 pkg. chocolate chips or 4½ oz.
chocolate bar

Melt caramels in water in top of double boiler. Arrange nuts in clusters on buttered cookie sheet; drop 1 teaspoon caramel on each nut cluster. Melt chocolate; spread over caramel.

NEVER-FAIL TOFFEE

Let making candy be an exciting experience.

2 c. sugar
1½ c. butter or margarine
2 Tbsp. water

½ c. slivered almonds
1 large bar milk chocolate, broken
in small pieces

Combine first 3 ingredients in heavy saucepan. Cook, stirring constantly, to soft crack stage. Pour immediately on unbuttered cookie sheet, spreading as thin as possible. Place chocolate on hot toffee; spread melting chocolate to cover toffee.

CHOCOLATE COCONUT CANDIES

¾ c. mashed potatoes
1 lb. flaked coconut (about 4 c.)
1 lb. confectioners sugar (about 4¾
c.)
1 tsp. almond or vanilla

1 (6 oz.) pkg. semi-sweet chocolate
bits
4 sq. (4 oz.) semi-sweet chocolate
⅓ paraffin bar (3x5 inches)

Combine first 4 ingredients. Drop by teaspoonfuls on waxed paper. Roll in balls. Refrigerate 1 hour. Melt the last 3 ingredients in double boiler to blend well. Dip balls in coating. With tongs, lift balls out of chocolate and place on wax paper. Place in refrigerator to harden; store in tight container.

CARAMEL APPLES

2 c. sugar or part brown
1 c. light corn syrup
½ stick margarine

1 tsp. vanilla
1 c. cream
Dash of salt

Cook sugar, syrup, cream, margarine and salt to medium hard ball stage. Let cool. Add vanilla. Dip apples in mixture and place on waxed paper.

CHINESE CHOCOLATES

2 pkg. Butterscotch chips (2 c.)
1 pkg. Chocolate Chips (1 c.)

1 lge. can Chinese Noodles
½ c. chopped nuts

Melt chips over hot water. Add Chinese Noodles and nuts. Mix thoroughly. Drop by teaspoon on waxed paper and let cool.

PECAN ROLLS

Fun to make and a challenge, a favorite of my family. Looks great, tastes wonderful.

2 c. white sugar
½ c. light corn syrup
½ c. water

1 lb. chopped pecans or enough to
cover rolls
2 eggs, separated

Cook sugar, water and syrup until forms soft ball stage. Take from burner and set aside. Beat 2 egg whites until stiff, then pour syrup mixture slowly into egg whites. Keep beating for 10 to 15 minutes. Set aside for a few minutes until you can handle with hands. Form into desired rolls, not too large.

Mix:

1 can Eagle Brand milk

½ c. light corn syrup

Cook and stir for 10 minutes. Take off heat and spread over each roll. Then drop in pecans and cover well. Then drop on wax paper.

EASY FONDANT

⅓ c. margarine
½ c. light corn syrup
1 lb. powdered sugar, sifted

⅛ tsp. flavoring oil
Desired food coloring

In 3 quart saucepan, heat margarine, corn syrup and ½ pound sugar over low heat until bubbly. Stir in remaining sugar. Remove from heat. Stir until mixture holds shape. Turn into greased pan. Cool until lukewarm. Knead until smooth. Add flavoring oil and coloring. Shape with lightly greased hands into balls, mint patties and etc.

TEXAS MILLIONAIRES

My favorite of the dipped chocolate candies. Professional quality. Delicious.

1 c. brown sugar, packed
1 c. white sugar
1 c. light corn syrup
2 sticks butter

2 c. canned milk
1 tsp. vanilla
2 c. pecan halves

Mix the first six ingredients, except 1 cup milk. Heat to hard rolling boil, slowly add second cup of milk, continually boiling and stirring constantly, cook to soft ball stage. This takes quite some time. Add 2 cups pecans, pour into large buttered dish. Store in refrigerator overnight. The next day, cut in desired shape and dip candy with toothpick.

Dip:

12 oz. chocolate chips
2 large milk chocolate Hershey's
bars

1¼ to 1½ sticks paraffin wax

Melt over double boiler, after melts, dip candy. Keep in cold place.

PEANUT BRITTLE

I usually make numerous pounds of peanut brittle for the holidays to give as gifts and just to share with family and friends. I always try to have an ample supply for "my man."

2 c. raw peanuts
2 c. white sugar
1 c. white corn syrup
½ c. water

2 Tbsp. margarine
1 tsp. vanilla
2 tsp. soda

Cook sugar, water and syrup to 280° on candy thermometer. Add margarine and peanuts. Stir to keep from scorching. Cook to 305°. Remove from fire, add vanilla. Add soda and stir *well*. Pour on well greased heavy duty aluminum foil. As it cools stretch to thin. When it cools break into pieces.

Note: Some thermometers vary. When the candy is ready to remove from stove it should be light brown in color.

PEANUT BUTTER EASTER EGGS

1½ c. margarine
½ lb. confectioners sugar
1 c. marshmallow creme

1 lb. confectioners sugar
1 c. peanut butter

Cream margarine and ½ pound confectioners sugar, then add marshmallow creme, peanut butter and the 1 pound confectioners sugar. Roll in balls or shape in eggs and coat with chocolate.

Variation: Can be put in pan, coat with chocolate. Cut in pieces.

DIVINITY

After sampling, I had to have this recipe. The recipe is excellent and turns out perfect. Shared to me from a friend Helen Bowden, you will enjoy making this candy. Color part of it for the holidays. Keeps very well in airtight container.

4 c. sugar
1 c. corn syrup
¾ c. water

3 egg whites, beaten stiff
1 c. nuts, chopped
1½ tsp. vanilla

Stir sugar, syrup and water over heat until sugar dissolves. Then cook without stirring to 255° or to hard ball stage. Pour in thin stream over egg whites with mixer at high speed. (Do not scrape pan.) Beat till holds shape and loses gloss. Add nuts and vanilla. Color if desired. Drop by teaspoon on foil.

SUGARED PEANUTS

2 cups unroasted peanuts
½ c. water

1 cup sugar

Cook and stir until mixture crystalizes and coats peanuts. About 10 minutes. Spread in a large buttered baking pan. Sprinkle with salt. Bake in 300 degree oven for 15 minutes. Lift and turn peanuts over with spatula. Bake 15 minutes more. Cool and store in airtight container.

HARD CANDY

Fun to make, nice for gifts. I use cinnamon oil and red food coloring, and wintergreen oil with green food coloring for the holidays.

2 c. sugar   1 tsp. candy flavoring oil
1 c. water   ½ tsp. food color
¾ c. light corn syrup   Powdered sugar

First, prepare 2 large cookie sheets by buttering and covering with ¼ inch powdered sugar. Make rows in sugar lengthwise with your finger about 1 inch apart. Combine sugar, water and corn syrup in heavy saucepan. Cook, stirring constantly, until sugar is dissolved. Then cook to 300° without stirring. Quickly remove from heat, stir in flavoring and food coloring, and pour into the rows you made in the cookie sheets. As soon as candy is cool enough to touch and barely begins to harden, cut with scissors into bite-size pieces. Allow to cool thoroughly and store in airtight container. This can also be used to make suckers. For thick candy use 1 cookie sheet.

CREAMY CHOCOLATE FUDGE

2 c. sugar   ⅛ tsp. salt
2 sq. baking chocolate   2 Tbsp. butter
2 Tbsp. corn syrup   1 tsp. vanilla
⅔ c. milk   ½ c. nuts

Combine first 5 ingredients; cook till firm ball in cold water. Let cool 15 minutes. Pour in bowl, beat on medium for 5 minutes. If hardens, add 1 tablespoon milk or 2 tablespoons corn syrup. Pour in buttered dish.

I can't believe I gained 10 pounds when I only ate 1 pound of fudge.

TAFFY PULL SUGAR CANDY

"One of my childhood favorites." When my sisters and I were very young we enjoyed making taffy, with our mother's help. When the taffy was cool enough to handle, we would butter our hands and really get with it, pulling it fast as we could, so that it would get white. As it would harden, we would twist it or leave it in long strips, then cut it into pieces and place on wax paper. Fun to do with children on New Year's Eve.

2 c. sugar   1 tsp. vanilla
1 c. water   1 cup of light corn syrup
A Tbsp. vinegar   Margarine for greasing pan and hands

Mix together and cook to hard boil stage, 265° to 270°. Do not stir. Pour in well greased platter until cool enough to work with. Lightly grease hands and pull taffy until white. Twist and cut into bite-size pieces. Set aside to harden on wax paper. Yields 1 pound.

Character is what we are when we think that no one is watching us

Low Calorie
Food

APPROXIMATE 100 CALORIE PORTIONS

Almonds (shelled)—12 to 15 nuts
Angel cake—1¾ inch cube
Apple—1 large
Apple pie—⅓ normal piece
Apricots—5 large
Asparagus—20 large stalks
Bananas—1 medium
Beans—⅓ cup canned baked
Beans—green string—2½ cups
Beets—1⅓ cups sliced
Bread—all kinds—slice ½ inch thick
Butter—1 tablespoon
Buttermilk—1⅛ cups
Cabbage—4 to 5 cups shredded
Cake—1¾ inch cube
Candy—1 inch cube
Cantaloupe—1 medium
Carrots—1⅔ cups
Cauliflower—1 small head
Celery—4 cups
Cereal—uncooked—¾ cup
Cheese—1⅛ inch cube
Cottage cheese—5 tablespoons
Cherries—sweet fresh—20 cherries
Cookies—1 to 3 inches in diameter
Corn—⅓ cup
Crackers—4 soda crackers
Crackers—graham—2½ crackers
Cream—thick—1 tablespoon
Cream—thin—4 tablespoons
Cream sauce—4 tablespoons
Dates—3 to 4
Doughnuts—½ doughnut
Eggs—1⅓ eggs
Fish—fat—size of 1 chop
Fish—lean—size of 2 chops
Flour—4 tablespoons
Frankfurter—1 small
French dressing—1½ tablespoons
Grapefruit—½ large
Grape juice—½ cup
Grapes—20 grapes
Gravy—2 tablespoons
Ice cream—½ cup
Lard—1 tablespoon
Lemons—3 large
Lettuce—2 large heads

Macaroni—¾ cup cooked
Malted milk—3 tablespoons
Marmalade and jelly—1 tablespoon
Marshmallows—5 marshmallows
Mayonnaise—1 tablespoon
Meat—cold sliced—⅛ inch slice
Meat—fat—size ½ chop
Meat—lean—size 1 chop
Milk—⅝ cup (regular)
Molasses—1½ tablespoons
Onions—3 to 4 Medium
Oranges—1 large
Orange juice—1 cup
Peaches—3 medium fresh
Peanut butter—1 tablespoon
Pears—2 medium fresh
Peas—¾ cup canned
Pecans—12 meats
Pie—¼ ordinary serving
Pineapple—2 slices 1 inch thick
Plums—3 to 4 large
Popcorn—1½ cups
Potatoes—sweet—½ medium
Potatoes—white—1 medium
Potato salad—1 cup
Prunes—dried 4 medium
Radishes—3 dozen red button
Raisins—¼ cup seeded or
   2 tablespoons seeded
Rhubarb—stewed and sweetened
   —½ cup
Rice—cooked ¾ cup
Rolls—1 medium
Rutabagas—1⅔ cups
Sauerkraut—2½ cups
Sherbet—4 tablespoons
Spinach—2½ cups
Squash—1 cup
Strawberries—1⅓ cups
Sugar—brown—3 tablespoons
Sugar—white—2 tablespoons
Tomatoes—canned—2 cups
Tomatoes—fresh—2 to 3 medium
Turnips—2 cups
Walnuts—8 to 16 meats
Watermelon—¾ slice 6 inches
   diameter

LOW CALORIE FOOD

WEIGHT WATCHER'S CHICKEN

Large can tomato juice
2 Tbsp. vinegar
8 Tbsp. Worcestershire sauce
3 tsp. mustard

Salt and pepper
2 tsp. sweetener or more to taste
1 or 2 chickens, cut up

Mix all ingredients well. Salt each piece of chicken, place into sauce in covered baking pan over roaster. Bake in 350° oven for 1½ hours.

To conquer without risk is to triumph without glory

LOW-CAL MEAT LOAF

...en
...urger
...opped fine
...opped celery
...c. chopped dill pickle
¼ c. chopped parsley (optional)
1 tsp. salt

¼ tsp. pepper
1 tsp. Worcestershire sauce
1 (4 oz.) can tomato sauce
½ tsp. prepared mustard
2 Tbsp. vinegar
1 Tbsp. honey

Place eggs, hamburger, onion, celery, dill pickle, parsley, salt and pepper, Worcestershire sauce and 1 can tomato sauce in bowl; mix well. Shape into loaf; place in shallow baking pan. Mix remaining 1 can tomato sauce, mustard, vinegar and honey in bowl; pour over loaf. Bake in preheated 350° oven for 1 hour or until done.

"A smile is a language understood by all persons."

DIABETIC CUSTARD

4 c. milk
4 eggs (whole)
1 Tbsp. sweetener

Nutmeg to taste
Pinch of salt
¾ c. raisins (optional)

Scald milk and sweetener and salt. Beat eggs and add to milk. Sprinkle with nutmeg. Set in a pan of cold water and bake at 350° for 30 minutes or until knife inserted in custard is clean.

"Seconds count, especially when on a diet."

CHEWY GRANOLA MUFFINS
(Impressive and a quaranteed success!)

1 c. granola
1 c. rolled oats
½ c. Bisquick
¼ c. Sugar Twin or sugar
½ c. raisins

¼ c. chopped pecans or other nuts
¼ c. cooking oil
2 eggs, beaten
⅔ c. milk

Mix first 6 ingredients in large bowl. Add oil, eggs and milk; stir until just moistened. Fill greased muffin tins ⅔ full. Bake in preheated oven for 15 to 20 minutes or until done; serve warm or cold.

"Little things can often be the biggest things in someone's day."

APPLESAUCE COOKIES
(No sugar)

1⅔ c. flour
½ tsp. salt
3 tsp. cinnamon
½ tsp. nutmeg
½ tsp. cloves
1 tsp. soda

1 c. applesauce
3 env. sweetener
1⅓ c. softened margarine
1 egg
½ c. raisins
½ c. chopped nuts

Chop raisins and cover with water. Let stand. Sift dry ingredients together. Mix margarine and eggs until light and fluffy. Add applesauce, sweetener and dry ingredients. Mix well. Stir in drained raisins and nuts. Drop by teaspoon on greased baking sheet. Bake at 350° for 20 to 25 minutes. Yields 2½ dozen.

PEACH WHIZ

4 fresh peaches, peeled and sliced
1 sliced banana

½ c. cream or evaporated milk

Puree in blender the peaches and bananas. Add cream and freeze in trays until mushy.

SHRIMP AND MUSHROOM SUPPER SALAD
(What a great way to diet!)

2 c. shrimp, cooked and chilled
4 c. shredded lettuce
½ lb. fresh mushrooms, thinly
    sliced
½ c. cucumber, thinly sliced

8 cherry tomatoes, halved
6 Tbsp. Italian salad dressing
Salt and pepper to taste
¼ tsp. dried oregano
Pinch of garlic powder (optional)

1. Slice shrimp in halves, or dice if large.
2. Combine all ingredients. Toss gently.
3. Serve immediately.

PEACH CRISP
(Low calorie)

Topping:

1 #2 can peaches
3 Tbsp. flour
3 Tbsp. sugar
⅛ tsp. cinnamon

Dash of salt
1½ Tbsp. butter or margarine
2 Tbsp. quick oats (uncooked)
Dash of nutmeg

Preheat oven to 400°. Pour peaches into a shallow 1 quart casserole. In a bowl, combine the dry ingredients for topping. Mix well. Cut in butter. Mix in oats. Sprinkle over peaches. Bake for 40 minutes or until lightly browned. Serve warm. Makes 6 servings. There are 107 calories in each serving.

On a diet, join the club.
It's the vogue, but here's the rub,
Food is tasteless, calorie counting is a bore,
If no will power you use, you'll end up as before.

"Im on the 300th day of
a 14 day diet!"

SUGARLESS OATMEAL COOKIES

Combine:

¼ c. salad oil or 1 stick margarine
1 egg
⅓ c. Sugar Twin

1 tsp. vanilla
½ tsp. salt
½ c. milk

Sift together:

1½ c. flour
½ tsp. cinnamon

1 tsp. baking powder

Combine all ingredients. Then add ½ cup quick oats and ½ cup raisins. Mix well and bake on greased cookie sheet at 350° for 15 minutes.

CHICKEN PILAF

¾ c. coarsely chopped celery
1 med. onion, chopped
2 tsp. butter
¼ c. chopped red sweet pepper

2 c. cooked rice
1½ c. chicken, chopped
Salt and pepper to taste

Sautee celery and onion in butter in skillet until tender. Add remaining ingredients. Simmer for 10 minutes, stirring constantly. Yield 4 servings about 290 calories each.

CALORIE COUNTER'S SPREAD

1 (8 oz.) container low fat cottage
  cheese
1 (2 oz.) jar diced pimientos,
  drained
1 Tbsp. chopped chives

½ tsp. Dijon mustard
¼ tsp. seasoned salt
Dash of ground black pepper
Saltine crackers

Combine cottage cheese, pimientos, chives, mustard, salt and pepper; mix thoroughly. Chill 1 hour or till serving time. Serve with saltine crackers. Makes about 1 cup spread.

LIGHT WEIGHT CHICKEN
(Chef's selection)

1 (3 lb.) chicken, disjointed
1 Tbsp. Blend No. 101 Chef's
  selection no salt seasoning
2 onions, rough cut
1 c. large diced celery

1 sliced zucchini
½ c. small diced green pepper
½ c. mushrooms and green onions
  (optional)

Place chicken skin side down in a heavy or non-stick skillet. Place ½ cup vegetables on the chicken and sprinkle No. 101 seasoning over all. Cook on very low heat for 40 minutes until chicken is brown on one side and moisture has been drawn out of vegetables (use no oil). Turn chicken, cover with remaining vegetables. Sprinkle with 2 tablespoons of low fat soy sauce (optional) and cook over low heat for 40 minutes. Do not cover skillet during cooking. Mushrooms may be added during last 15 minutes of cooking. Serve on platter with fresh side salad with vinegar dressing.

♡ SUGAR FREE STRAWBERRY PIE

2 env. sugar free strawberry gelatin
1½ c. boiling water
Few drops of artificial sweetener
1 Tbsp. lemon juice
1½ c. strawberry diet pop

2 c. fresh strawberries, mashed
2 egg whites
¼ tsp. cream of tartar
1 env. D'Zerta whipped topping mix
1 (9 inch) baked pie shell

Dissolve gelatin in boiling water. Add artificial sweetener. Add lemon juice. Add pop. Chill until partially set. Fold in strawberries. Beat egg whites and cream of tartar to stiff peaks. Prepare topping mix according to package directions. Fold egg whites and ¾ cup topping mix into gelatin mixture. Fill pie shell. Remaining whipped topping may be used as a garnish. Any remaining mixture can be used as a pudding, or as a salad.

DIABETIC JELLY

2 c. unsweetened grape juice
1 c. water
½ c. tapioca

Artificial sweetener equivalent to
3 c. sugar

Mix together and let stand 5 minutes to soften tapioca. Bring to hard boil and boil one minute. Skim off foam and seal in sterilized jars. Can use any flavor juice.

NO CALORIE SOUP

1 head cabbage
6 onions
1 large can tomatoes

1 bunch celery
1 large green pepper
4 beef bouillon cubes (optional)

Cover with water and bring to a boil. Cook for one hour or until vegetables are tender.

DIET DIP

1 c. cream style cottage cheese
2 Tbsp. skim milk
1 Tbsp. chopped green pepper

1 Tbsp. radishes
1 Tbsp. chopped green onion
⅛ tsp. celery salt

Beat cottage cheese and milk until creamy. Stir in other ingredients and chill one hour. One cup yield. One-third cup equals 85 calories.

NO SUGAR COOKIES

2 c. flour
½ c. nuts, chopped
½ c. raisins
½ c. orange juice

1 tsp. orange peel
½ tsp. salt
½ tsp. cinnamon
1 egg

Mix all together. Drop 1 inch apart. Bake in 375° oven for 20 minutes.

LOW CALORIE CHILI

1 lb. ground turkey
   or veal.
2 16 oz. cans tomatoes
1 chopped onion
1 small can mushroom pieces

1 can kidney beans
chili powder
2 pkg's sweetner

Brown Turkey, add rest of ingredients and simmer for a few minutes.

MARINATED SALMON STEAKS

Chose 1 inch salmon steaks for this tried and tested recipe by a friend Ruby Bloom from Prescott, Ar. Even if you're not a seafood cook, try this easy way to make a beautiful seafood entree. The flavor shines through the light marinade. For an extra touch, garnish with parsley.

Use salmon steaks.

Marinade Sauce:

Lemon juice   **Minced garlic**
Oregano   **Snipped fresh dill**

Pour marinade sauce over the steaks. Preheat broiler pan about 15 minutes. Oil the rack before placing the marinade steaks on it. Broil about 5 minutes on each side. Baste with remaining marinade.

Sittin' and wishin' won't improve our fate;
The Lord provides the fishes, but we gotta
Dig the bait ...

TEENY-Weeny Applesauce Cupcakes (Delicious)

½ c. margarine   ½ t. nutmeg
1 egg   ¼ t. cloves
2 t. Sweet & Low   ¼ t. ginger
¾ c. flour   1 c. Unsweetened
1 t. baking soda   applesauce
¼ t. salt   2 t. vanilla
1 t. cinnamon   ⅓ c. raisins
                            ⅓ c. chopped nuts

Cream margarine until fluffy. Beat egg and sweetener until thick and lemon colored, add to margarine and mix well. Sift together all the dry ingredients. Add to margarine mixture alternately with applesauce, starting and ending with dry. Blend well after each addition. Add vanilla, blend in raisins and nuts. Pour into tiny cupcake tart tins, filling ⅔ full. Bake 15 to 20 minutes or until tester comes out clean. Makes 30 cupcakes. 71 calories each.

Left to Right - Bill, Greg, Brad, Dad, Mom, Jim, Tim, Doug

THEY ARE GROWN—UP NOW.

Family ties are precious bonds
   that passing time endears,
For they begin with memories
   of your happy childhood years—

Family ties are growing bonds
   nourished by love and laughter
And a thousand everyday events
   that are cherished ever after—

Family ties are lasting bonds
   that are woven in each heart
To keep a family close in thought
   together or apart!

Author Unknown

Odds and Ends

TO QUICK-FREEZE VEGETABLES

Vegetables for freezing are prepared as for cooking, then blanched (scalded) and packed dry, or with the brine. The dry pack is less trouble and is satisfactory for all vegetables except green peppers.

Blanching vegetables is important because it minimizes loss of flavor and color. To blanch in boiling water, put about one pound of vegetables in a fine-mesh wire basket with a wire cover to hold food under the water and lower into rapidly boiling water, enough to cover food. Cover the kettle and then COUNT THE TIME RECOMMENDED FOR EACH vegetable. After blanching, chill quickly and thoroughly, plunge the vegetables into ice water, or hold under cold running water. When completely chilled, remove and drain, and PACK AT ONCE.

VEGETABLE	HOW PREPARED	BLANCHING
ASPARAGUS	Wash, cut, sort into groups according to thickness of stalk. Blanch, chill, pack.	3 to 4 minutes in boiling water, depending on size.
BEANS, GREEN AND WAX	Wash, stem, slice, cut or leave whole. Blanch, chill, pack.	Cut: 2 minutes in boiling water. Whole: 2½ minutes in boiling water.
BEANS, LIMA	Shell, wash, blanch, chill. Remove white beans, which may be used for cooking. Pack.	1 to 2 minutes in boiling water, depending on size.
CARROTS	Remove tops, wash, scrape. Slice lengthwise or crosswise as preferred, or leave small carrots whole.	Whole: 4½ minutes in boiling water. Sliced: 3 minutes in boiling water.
CAULIFLOWER	Break heads into flowerets about 1 inch across. Wash, blanch, chill, pack.	3 to 4 minutes in boiling water.
CORN, ON COB	Husk, trim away silk and spots. Wash, blanch, chill, pack.	7 minutes in boiling water for slender ears. 9 for medium, 11 for large.
CORN, KERNELS	Same as corn on cob. After chilling, cut off kernels and pack.	
GREENS Beet, Chard, Kale, Mustard, Spinach, Collards, etc.	Wash, discard bad leaves, tough stems. Blanch, chill, pack.	2 minutes in boiling water.
PEAS	Shell, sort, blanch, chill, pack.	1 to 2 minutes in boiling water, depending on size.
PEPPERS, GREEN	Wash, cut away seeds, slice. Blanch, pack in brine of 1 tsp. salt to 1 c. cold water.	3 minutes in boiling water.

ODDS AND ENDS

CINNAMON APPLES

A recipe, that is a special family tradition at Christmas for cinnamon apples, was shared to me from a friend Phyllis McBroom, who lives in beautiful Prescott, Ar.

2 c. sugar
2 c. water
1 pkg. cinnamon drops

Red cake coloring
1 doz. yellow delicious apples

Cook apples in above mixture and place In large casserole dish. Thicken remaining liquid with cornstarch and pour over apples. Refrigerate and serve.

A bell is not a Bell
til you ring it
A song is not a Song
until you sing it
Love is not Love
til you give it.

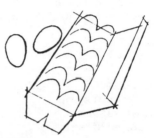

BASIC DEVILED EGGS

6 eggs
¼ c. mayonnaise
1 tsp. vinegar

1 tsp. prepared mustard
½ tsp. salt
Dash of pepper

Boil eggs. Shell and slice lengthwise. Put yolks in a bowl and mash. Add remaining ingredients and then re-stuff eggs, topping with paprika.

SPICED PECANS

1 lb. pecans
1 egg white

1 Tbsp. water

Beat egg white and water until frothy but not stiff. Turn nuts into egg white mixture for coating.

Mix together:

1 c. sugar
1 tsp. salt

1 tsp. cinnamon

Mix sugar mixture with egg and nut mixture. Place on well greased cookie sheet. Put in 250° oven for 1 hour. Turn every 15 minutes.

QUICK GUACAMOLE

Mash two ripe Avacados
2 tsp. Lemon Juice

1 tsp. garlic powder
½ c. chunky salsa

Mix ingredients together and let set in refrigerator to blend flavors.

FROSTED PECANS

If you love pecans and nibbling, this is for you!

½ c. butter
2 egg whites (at room temperature)

1 c. light brown sugar
1 lb. large pecans

1. Melt butter in 9x13 inch pan in oven. Set aside.
2. Beat egg whites until very stiff. Gradually add sugar until mixture is thick and smooth. Take time doing this so the meringue has body.
3. Fold in pecans until they are thoroughly coated.
4. Drop mixture by spoonfuls into the pan with the melted butter.
5. Bake. Every ten minutes gently turn and separate the nuts using small spatula so they are evenly covered with butter.
6. Cool in the pan.
Bake at 300° for 1 hour.

CARAMEL CORN

2 sticks butter
½ c. white corn syrup
2 c. brown sugar
¼ tsp. cream of tartar

1 tsp. salt
1 tsp. soda
6 to 7 qt. popped corn

Mix butter, syrup and brown sugar; bring to a boil. Let boil for 6 minutes and keep stirring. Take off heat and add cream of tartar, salt and soda; stir until foaming. Pour on popcorn and bake at 250° for 1 hour, turning lightly with spatula every 15 minutes.

PEOPLE SEED

A no cook easy snack that is very habit forming.

Raisins
Chocolate chips
Popped popcorn
Peanuts

Sunflower seeds
Chopped dates
Small pretzels
Chinese noodles

OVEN READY SOUPER BURGERS

A very easy, but good time saving recipe.

1 lb. ground beef
½ pkg. dry onion soup mix
1 can cream of mushroom soup

1 c. grated Cheddar cheese
Hamburger buns

Brown ground beef. Drain grease. Add dry onion soup and mushroom soup (do not heat). Spoon mixture on hamburger buns. Sprinkle with grated cheese. Wrap each bun in foil and freeze. When ready to serve, remove from frezer 20 minutes before baking in 350° oven for 30 minutes. Depending on how much filling you like, this will make eight hamburgers.

SWEET NOTHINS

Let your children help you!! Dora Mae Cravens, from Huntsville, Mo., Home Economics teacher, along with her students, created this tasty fun to make "roll up" treat. Flatten slices of bread with a rolling pin - spread with your favorite jelly or jam. Roll up jelly roll style and wrap in Handi-Wrap. Refrigerate for an hour or so and slice in 3 to 4 pieces. Dip in a thin or medium fritter batter. Fry, drain and roll in confectioners sugar.

No family hides its secrets well
Whose children shine at show and tell.

FRITTER BATTER
(For onion rings, etc.)

½ c. milk
2 eggs
1 tsp. salt

1 c. flour
1 tsp. baking powder

Mix well the milk, eggs, oil and salt. Add the flour and baking powder. May thin out with milk if necessary.

GRAHAM CRACKER ICE CREAM SANDWICHES

1 small pkg. instant pudding and pie
    filling (any flavor)
1¼ c. whipped cream, Cool Whip or
    Dream Whip

About 32 graham crackers

In a small bowl, combine pudding with milk. Mix on low speed till thick, about 2 minutes. Chill till set, about 5 minutes. Fold in whipped cream or topping. Spread ¼ cup pudding mixture on 16 graham crackers and wrap individually with plastic wrap. Freeze until firm.

Enthusiasm in large measure is an indispensable ingredient of happy living.

SOME MORE SMORES

Excellent for camping, good for partys for children, easy to make.

8 graham cracker squares
2 milk chocolate candy bars

8 large marshmallows

Place 4 graham cracker squares on napkin-lined paper plate. Top each cracker with 2 chocolate squares and 1 marshmallow. Microwave on HIGH for 40 seconds. Place remaining crackers on top. Let stand for 1 minute. Yields 4 servings.

Note: If camping or having a wiener roast, just melt the marshmallows and assemble with graham cracker and chocolate candy bar.

OUR FAVORITE RECIPE

2 well scrubbed kids
1 buttered-up daddy

1 fist full of dough

Place in well greased car and head for the nearest restaurant.

INDIVIDUAL PIZZAS

½ lb. hamburger
1 tsp. oregano
1 garlic clove, minced or ½ tsp.
    powder
1 pkg. (12) refrigerated biscuits

1 small can tomato paste
1 c. shredded Cheddar cheese
¼ c. grated Parmesan cheese
Olives, mushrooms for top

Brown and drain hamburger. Add remaining ingredients. Except the biscuits. Take biscuits and pat out; top with hamburger mixture. Top with the cheese. Bake until biscuits are done.

Optimism is the faith that leads to achievement.

STUFFED PEPPERS

Cook:

1 lb. ground beef
1 c. chopped onion

1 clove garlic, chopped
2 tsp. chili powder

Add:

1 tsp. salt
½ tsp. pepper

2 cans tomato soup

Cook a little more and then add:

½ lb. cheese

1½ c. cooked rice

Stir until cheese is melted and put in cooled peppers. Cook cleaned peppers in boiling salted water not more than 3 minutes. Drain and cool, and then stuff with cooled mixture. Freeze if you like. Remove frozen peppers and place in pan in oven and cover with foil. Bake at 400° for 30 to 45 minutes.

POP CORN BALLS

1 c. sugar
1 T. butter
½ c. white Karo Syrup

3 T. water
3 quarts popped popcorn

Boil sugar, syrup, butter and water until it spins a long thread. Pour over popped corn and shape into balls.

PANCAKES

A recipe for her "special pancakes," shared to me from my mother-in-law, Ola Remole from Potomac, Il., adding the homemade maple syrup to make them complete.

2 beaten eggs	1½ c. flour
½ tsp. soda	½ tsp. salt
1 c. buttermilk	

Beat eggs until light. Add baking soda and stir. Add buttermilk. Add the flour and salt. Add enough flour to make right consistency for frying. Fry on oiled medium hot griddle.

Maple Syrup:

2 c. sugar	1 tsp. maple flavor
1 c. water	1 Tbsp. butter

Stir ingredients until dissolved. Bring to a boil and cook together for 1 minute.

Somehow, not only for Christmas
But all the long year through
The joy that you give to others
Is the joy that comes back to you.

CRUSTY POTATO TIDBITS

2 lb. hot, cooked russet potatoes	1 c. grated Parmesan cheese
2 Tbsp. milk	2 Tbsp. minced green onion
3 Tbsp. butter or margarine	2 eggs, beaten
¼ tsp. salt	3 to 4 c. corn flakes, coarsely
⅛ tsp. pepper	crushed

Peel potatoes; mash with milk, butter, salt and pepper. Stir in cheese and green onion; mix well. Shape mixture into balls about 1 inch in diameter. Dip potato balls in eggs, then roll in corn flakes. Place on greased baking sheet and bake at 400° for 10 minutes or until balls are hot and crusty. Makes about 70 appetizer balls.

NOODLES

There is something special about homemade noodles. You will enjoy making this easy recipe.

Beat 3 egg yolks and 1 whole egg until very light. Beat in 3 tablespoons cold water and ½ teaspoon salt. Stir in 2 cups Gold Medal flour. Divide dough in 3 parts. Roll out on floured surface. Let dry on cloth or area that they can dry well. Roll up and slice to ⅛ inch thickness for narrow noodles and ½ inch for wide noodles. Shake out and they are ready to drop in boiling broth. Cook ½ hour or until tender on medium heat, stirring occasionally.

Learning is a treasure for eternity.

TOASTED COCONUT

Makes 1 cup. Toasted coconut is an elegant accessory for many different foods. Sprinkle it over fruit cup, serve it for a smashing dessert over whipped toppings or coconut pie with whipped topping.

Use 1 (4 ounce) can flaked coconut. Preheat oven to 300° and line with foil. Spread coconut evenly on foil sheet and bake, stirring occasionally, until flakes are lightly browned, about 10 minutes. Cool and store in a tight container.

PRALINE SAUCE
(Very delicious over ice cream!)

½ c. butter
1½ c. firmly packed brown sugar
2 Tbsp. plus 1 tsp. light corn syrup
½ tsp. burnt sugar flavoring
  (optional)

½ c. whipping cream
⅓ c. chopped pecans

In medium saucepan, melt butter; stir in brown sugar and syrup. Bring to boil. Cook until sugar is dissolved, stirring constantly. Stir in whipping cream and bring to a boil again. Remove from heat and stir in nuts. Serve warm over ice cream. Store in refrigerator. Makes 2 cups.

PICKLED OKRA

3 c. white vinegar
3 c. water

5 Tbsp. canning salt
okra (sliced or whole)

Heat the above to real hot. Pack okra in hot jars.

Add:

½ red pepper, chopped
1 clove garlic, chopped

¼ tsp. mustard seed
1 tsp. dried dill seed

Pour liquid over and seal. Set at least 1 month before opening.

MICROWAVED PEANUT BRITTLE

1 c. sugar
½ c. white corn syrup
1 c. salted peanuts

1 t. butter
1 t. vanilla extract
1 tsp. baking soda

In one 1 qt. casserole stir together the sugar and white corn syrup. Microwave 4 minutes on high. Stir in the peanuts and microwave 4-5 minutes on high. Add butter and vanilla and microwave 2 minutes. Peanuts will be lightly browned and syrup very hot. Add 1 teaspoon baking soda. Stir until light and foamy. Pour mixture onto lightly greased cookie sheet or buttered heavy foil. Let cool ½ to 1 hour. When cool, break into small pieces and store in air tight container.

ZUCCHINI PICKLES

My sister Pat and her husband Hugh enjoy raising zucchini in their garden. Pat shared some of these pickles with me and also the recipe. When I served these to company, they really enjoyed them, and surprised to find out they were made with zucchini. When canned, they really look like pickles, when chilled in refrigerator, they are crisp like a pickle. You will be proud to serve them.

4 qt. zucchini, sliced but not pared   1½ tsp. turmeric
6 medium white onions   1½ tsp. celery seed
2 medium green peppers   3 tsp. mustard seed
5 c. sugar   ½ c. salt
3 c. white cider vinegar

Slice zucchini in ¼ inch slices. Add sliced onions, green peppers and the salt. Cover the ice water for 3 hours. Drain well but do not rinse. Combine sugar, spices and vinegar, bring to boil, then add zucchini mixture, return to boil and simmer ½ hour. Can serve hot.

FREEZER PICKLES
(Crisp and crunchy)

7 c. sliced cucumbers   1 tsp. salt
1 c. sliced onions

Let the above stand for 2 hours, to bring juice out. Bring to a boil the following and then let cool:

1 c. vinegar   2 c. sugar
1 tsp. celery seed   ½ tsp. mustard

Then drain water off of cucumbers (not super dry). Pour boiled mixture over cucumbers and onions and refrigerate for 2 days before freezing.

RECIPE SAVER

I clip them from the magazines
and from newspapers too,
I gather them from neighbors, friends ...
and this is nothing new.
I take them down from the radio
and file them all away,
New dishes every day.

What fancy menus do I plan
From all the recipes;
or I'll bake this and I'll cook that ...
The family will I please,
And yet somehow I find myself
Repeating, so it seems,
The same old meals I've done for years ...
The rest are in my dreams.

CARAMEL CORN CHEX

½ c. margarine
1 c. brown sugar
¼ c. white corn syrup
½ tsp. salt

¼ tsp. baking soda
10 c. Corn Chex, Wheat Chex, or
   Rice Chex

Boil margarine, brown sugar, white corn syrup and salt for 5 minutes. Remove from burner and add baking soda. Pour mixture over Corn Chex, stirring as you pour. Bake in a roaster pan at 200 ° for 60 minutes. Stir every 15 minutes. Turn out on a cookie sheet; cool.

Common honesty isn't a spectular quality. But it wears like iron.

OYSTER CRACKER SNACK
(An interesting good snack)

2 (10 oz.) pkg. oyster crackers
1 c. vegetable oil
1 oz. pkg. dry original Hidden Valley
   Ranch dressing

3 tsp. dry dill weed
½ tsp. garlic salt
1 tsp. lemon pepper

Pour oil over crackers and coat. Mix all dry ingredients, stir and sprinkle over crackers, stir and pour into large pan and let set for 30 minutes.

SUMMER SAUSAGE

A recipe from the Heart of Missouri from Cindy Fodree, a genuine country wife and homemaker.

¼ tsp. pepper
1 tsp. garlic salt
¼ tsp. onion salt
1 tsp. mustard seed

2 Tbsp. Morton's Tender-Quick
2 tsp. liquid smoke
1 c. water

Add to 2 pounds deerburger or ground chuck. Mix together and cover. Refrigerate overnight. Shape in two rolls the size of a half dollar. Wrap in heavy foil and turn up the ends. Place on cookie sheet. Bake in 350° oven for 30 minutes. Reduce heat to 250° and bake 30 minutes more. Drain well.

SAUSAGE AND CHEESE BALLS

1 lb. mild sausage
2 c. shredded Cheddar cheese

3 c. Bisquick

Mix together and make into small balls. Bake in 350° oven for 18 minutes.

What you think of yourself is much more important than what others think of you.

JO ELLEN'S SUPREME NACHOS

O'LAY!

1 lb ground beef or
  shredded chicken (cooked)
1 can refried beans
1 pkg Taco seasoning
½ lb monterey jack cheese
  (shredded)

½ lb cheddar cheese
  (shredded)
Tortilla chips
Optional: lettuce, tomatoes, black olives,
  sour cream, jalepeno peppers, gua-
  camole

Brown ground beef and drain. Mix taco seasoning into refried beans and add enough salsa to make a spreadable consistency. Place chips on a large platter in a single layer. Spread bean mixture over chips evenly. Next comes the layer of cheeses. Heat in oven until cheese melts and place any of the optional items on top to your own taste. Enjoy!

ROY'S 7 POUND NUT GOODIE CANDY

Roy McMahan, a friend from Potomac, Illinois, is well known for his touch of making delicious homemade candy. A great candy for the Holidays.

6 c. sugar
2 sticks butter
1½ lbs. light Karo syrup

1 lg. & 1 sm. can Carnation milk
8 c. nutmeats

Cook all ingredients (except nutmeats) to soft ball stage. Take off heat and beat, beat, beat. Add nutmeats. Pour in greased 8 x 13 x 2 inch pan. Let set until set. Turn out and cut. Keep in tight plastic container. I have been making this candy for over 40 years. The secret to success is beating it just right. Here is the easy way to do it. I put it in the sink with cold water and beat taking it in and out of water. I beat it until when I take some on a spoon and let it pour back in the pan and write Roy. If I can still see the R when I get the Y done, it is ready to put in nuts Not beating it long enough causes it not to set. Overbeating will cause it to crumble.

JELLO DIVINITY

3 c. sugar
¾ c. light corn syrup
¾ c. water
dash of salt

2 egg whites
1 pkg. Jello, any flavor
½ c. nuts, chopped

Cook sugar, syrup and water to hard crack stage. Cover when 1st begins to boil to disslove sugar. Beat egg whites until frothy. Add jello., beat until stiff. ADD HOT SYRUP slowly, beating until candy loses its gloss. Drop by teaspoons on waxed paper.

OLD FASHIONED FUDGE

My favorite

4 Tbsp. Cocoa
2 c. sugar
1 c. milk

2 Tbsp. butter or margarine
1 tsp. vanilla
½ c. black walnuts or peacans (optional)

Place cocoa in saucepan, rub into smooth paste by adding part of the cup milk. Add sugar, butter the size of walnut and remaining milk. Cook until forms of soft ball when dropped in cold water. Remove from heat, add vanilla. Beat until just thick enough to pour into buttered pan. Cool and cut into 1 inch squares. If using nuts, add when just starting to get thick. Note: Do not let get to thick before pouring into pan.

FROSTED CREAMS

A 3rd generation recipe, one you will enjoy. Handed down from mother with Love.

1 c. sugar
1 c. shortening
½ c. dark Karo syrup
1 c. boiling coffee
2 eggs
4 c. flour

2 t. soda
1 t. cinnamon
1 t. ginger
1 t. cloves
1 ½ c. raisins, cooked
1 c. nuts, chopped

Sift flour, measure, sift again with dry ingredients. Cream sugar, shortening, add beaten eggs. Add syrup, then flour and coffee. Add rasins, nuts last. Spread on 2 cookie sheets with sides. Bake in 350 degree oven until very light brown, approximately 10 minutes. Glaze with powder sugar icing promptly after removing from oven.

PECAN PRALINES

1 package instant pudding
1 c. sugar
½ c. brown sugar

½ c. evaporated milk
1 Tbsp. butter or margarine
1 ½ c. pecan pieces

Mix pudding, sugar, milk and butter in pan. Cook over low heat until sugar is disolved and mixture boils. Cook gently, stirring frequently until a soft ball is formed in cold water. Add nuts and mix well. Remove from heat, heat until mixture begins to thicken. Drop by teaspoon onto waxed paper and let set.

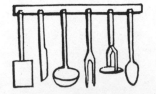

CHOCOLATE CHIP COOKIES

This recipe is from our daughter-in-law, Kathy Remole. Family and friends rave over her chocolate chip cookies.

2¼ c. all-purpose flour
1 t. baking soda
1 t. salt
½ c. butter
½ c. crisco

¾ c. sugar
¾ c. firmly packed brown sugar
2 t, vanilla extract
2 eggs
12 oz. semi sweet chocolate
   chips
1 c. chopped nuts

Preheat oven to 375 degrees. In small bowl, combine flour, baking soda and salt. set aside. In large bowl combine butter, sugars and vanilla extract; beat until creamy. Beat in eggs. Gradually add flour mixture and mix well. Stir in chocolate chips and nuts. Drop by rounded tablespoons onto an ungreased cookie sheet. Bake 9 to 11 minutes. Mmm Good!

OATMEAL COOKIES

The old fashion kind

2 c. raisins
1½ c. water
1 c. margarine or crisco
1½ sugar
1 c. hot raisin water
2 eggs

3½ c. flour
2 t. soda
4 well beaten eggs
2 t. baking powder
4 c. rolled oats

Boil raisins and 1½ cups water for 3 minutes. Cream margarine and sugar. Add 1 c. hot raisin water and soda. Mix well; Add 4 beaten eggs, baking powder and flour. Mix well and add rolled oats and raisins. Drop on a greased cookie sheet by teaspoonfuls and bake in a 375 oven until golden brown. Sprinkle with colored sugar. Makes 5 dozen.

PATTY'S NO BAKE COOKIES

2 c. sugar
½ c. cocoa

¼ c. margarine
½ c. milk

Cook these ingredients to a boil and let boil for a while. Add the remaining ingredients while hot.

½ c. peanut butter
3 c. quick Quaker oats

½ c. nuts (optional)
1 Tbsp. vanilla

Blend and drop on waxed paper. Cool.

ALMOND CRUNCH CAKE

Super delicious!

Cake

1½ c. sifted flour
1½ c. sugar, divided
8 eggs, seperated
¼ c. cold water

1 Tbsp. lemon juice
2 t. vanilla
1 t. cream of tarter
1 t. salt

Almond Brittle Topping

1½ c. sugar
¼ teaspoon instant coffee
¼ c. light corn syrup
¼ c. hot water

2½ c. heavy cream
2 tablespoons sugar
2 tablespoons vanilla
almonds, blanched halved
    and toasted.

Cake; Sift together flour and ¾ cup sugar. Make a well in the center, add egg yolks, water, lemon juice, vanilla and beat until smooth. Beat egg whites, cream of tarter, and salt just until soft peaks form. Add remaining sugar, 2 tablespoons at a time, continuing to beat until stiff. Fold flour mixture gently into egg whites. Pour batter into a 10 inch tube pan or two 2 quart baking pans. Cut carefully through the batter, going around 5 or 6 times, with knife, to break air bubbles. Bake at 350 degrees for 50 to 55 minutes or until top springs back when lightly touched. Invert pan 1 hour or until cool. Remove cake and split in 4 equal layers if using a tube pan. Make either 2 or 4 layers if using baking pans.

Almond Brittle Topping: Combine sugar, coffee, syrup, and water in a saucepan, stirring well. Cook to hard crack stage, 290 degrees, remove from heat, and add soda. Stir vigorously until mixture blends and pulls away from sides of pan. Quickly pour into a shallow baking sheet. Do not grease sheet. Let stand until cool. Knock out of pan and crush candy with a rolling pin into small chunks. Whip cream and fold in sugar and vanilla. Spread ½ of cream between cake layers and remainder over top and sides. Cover top and sides with candy, lightly pressing into cream. Decorate with almonds. Do not press candy and almonds into cream more than 6 hours.

Don't be afraid of a new idea.
Even a turtle knows he must stick out
                    his neck if he is to get anywhere.

BUTTERMILK POUND CAKE

In a large mixing bowl, beat ½ cup (1 cube) butter or margarine until creamy. Gradually add 2½ cups sugar, beating until mixture is light and fluffy. Beat in 4 eggs, one at a time, beating well after each addition. Sift all-purpose flour, measure 3 cups, sift again with ¼ teaspoon soda. Beat into creamed mixture alternately with 1 cup buttermilk mixed with 2 teaspoons almond extract, and the grated peel of an orange and 1 small lemon (begin and end with dry ingredients). Pour into a greased and floured 10-inch tube cake pan. Bake in a moderate oven (350 degrees) for 1 hour or until toothpick comes out clean. Allow to cool in pan for 5 minutes. Turn out onto wire rack to continue cooling.

MY DO-IT-MYSELF DIET.

I've gained ten pounds, I'm overweight
I'm going on a diet!
"I have a good one, " said my friend,
"I know you'll like it, try it!"

I took my friend's advice to heart
And fared just fine till Sunday
Invited out for lunch, I vowed,
"I'll start my diet Monday!"

Lois Charles

Index

FAVORITE RECIPES
FROM MY COOKBOOK

Recipe Name	Page Number